Sew Your Own Riding Clothes

SEW YOUR OWN RIDING CLOTHES

LINNÉA A. SHEPPARD

Breakthrough

Breakthrough Publications
Ossining, New York 10562
Printed in the United States of America

Library of Congress Catalog Card Number: 94-78486

ISBN: 0-914327-56-9

00 99 98 97 96 95 94 5 4 3 2 1

Text design by Virginia Pope
Fashion drawings by Gayle Vanwely MacKenzie
Sewing illustrations by Laurie Baker-McNeile
Cover design by Jean Criscola

CONTENTS

PREFACE

In 1985, my love of sewing and horseback riding led to my starting SuitAbility, a company that sells patterns for riding apparel. I had been sewing my own skiwear and wanted to sew my own riding apparel, too.

I have found that there are lots of people like me, who really enjoy combining two favorite pastimes and who like to save money as well. I've talked to thousands of customers over the years, and every week someone comes up with a new question. Customers wanted and needed to know all sorts of information that just could not be included in pattern guide sheets. I wrote this book to provide that information, and I've tried to answer common questions and address topics that many people seem interested in.

This book is for those who are already sewing riding items or who would like to try it. It is intended to help those with all levels of sewing experience. Whatever garment you choose to sew, I'm sure you'll experience the pleasure and pride of using your own creativity and skill to produce something of value.

I'd like to thank my editor, Rhona Johnson, who had to deal with an author moving cross-country during book deadlines; Alexis Antes, who effectively ran SuitAbility while I wrote this book; Laurie Baker-McNeile, Carol Zahn, and Gail MacKenzie for their invaluable contributions; Charlene Strickland, Gloria Nelson of Korral Kreations, and Isabelle Lott of Pattern Works, International, for answering my many questions about apparel and sewing; my SuitAbility customers, whose questions and

comments over the years have provided my real educa-
tion; my family and friends who have always supported
my efforts; and finally, my horses, Penalize and Conan, for
being patient "test" subjects.

I dedicate this book to my mother, Carol L. Sheppard,
who taught me to love sewing, to my father, Stanton V.
Sheppard, for his many forms of support, and also to my
husband, Randall W. Holt, who patiently listened to my
endless discussions about this project.

Sew Your Own Riding Clothes

CHAPTER 1

WHY SEW YOUR OWN?

I have talked to many people over the years who want to sew their own riding clothes. Often the conversation has gone like this: "My daughter wants to show hunt seat this year in Morgan classes and she needs the complete outfit. It's going to be expensive to buy, but, although I am not a horsey person myself, I can sew. Perhaps I can make her an outfit. I just don't know where to start."

Sewing your own riding apparel makes sense for many reasons. The obvious one is cost. When a major horse magazine does a Western show apparel makeover for **only $350**, it's easy to see that big savings are possible for those of us that can sew. A visit to a tack store to price riding jackets and breeches is enough to send you screaming to the sewing machine.

Another reason to sew your own riding clothes is to get the correct fit. A correct fit is crucial for both show and schooling apparel. In the show ring, a well-fitting outfit can mean the difference between being in the ribbons and being shown the gate. In performance events, you do not want to be distracted by uncomfortable garments. Knowing that you look well put together can only help your performance. For those that are in the saddle day in and day out, fit can be synonymous with function. Most ready-to-wear is sized for the "average" person (if such a person exists!), and worse yet, clothing for hunt and dressage riders is sized for the average European person. For many of us, the **only** way to get a correctly fitted garment is to have a custom-made one.

How many times have you had an idea in your head for the perfect show outfit, but found nothing vaguely resembling it in any store? You know just what colors would look best on you and your horse, but you end up settling for something else because that's all your local tack shop stocks. Or you'd love to buy a custom-sewn outfit, but just don't have the money. The solution is no farther away than your own sewing machine. You can have the exact combination of fabric, design features, and color that you want, if you sew it yourself. If you want to make riding clothes, you need to ask and answer the following questions:

✔ What pattern should I buy?
✔ What fabric should I use?
✔ How difficult will it be for me to sew?
✔ How do I get a good fit?
✔ What sewing techniques will I need to use?

In this book I will try to give you the answers to these questions and much more. Besides discussing how to get started, I will also describe a wide range of riding clothes including hunt seat, dressage, saddle seat, Western, and pleasure riding apparel. For each type of garment, I will give you an overview of the latest styles. Special fitting information will include techniques for alterations commonly needed for the various types of garments discussed in this book. I will give you help with selecting and using fabrics and notions, including mail-order sources for hard-to-find items such as stretch fabrics, leather, and outerwear supplies. Special sewing techniques will be explained. I will also give you some custom-styling ideas as a starting place for your own individual creative efforts. I also describe how to convert patterns to individual taste. You'll also find simple patterns for accessories.

Although this book is meant to be used with commercial patterns (pattern companies are listed in Appendix II), you'll find tips and advice that you won't find in commercial patterns. You'll learn how the techniques for sewing riding apparel differ from those for sewing regular clothes. I will give you some basic guidance on proper show apparel–when to wear what–in Appendix I. Finally, I list helpful books and publications which will expand your knowledge of both sewing and choosing riding apparel.

To Make or to Buy?

Though saving money is a major motivation to sew your own riding apparel, there's no guarantee that a sewn item will be cheaper than a bought item. Many discount catalogs sell show clothes and schooling apparel for less than the cost of sewing them, especially if you factor in the time you'll spend. You definitely save money, however, if you compare ready-made items and sewn items of the same quality. I made myself a hunt coat using exquisite $50/yard Italian wool gabardine, which ended up costing more than low-end hunt coats I've seen in catalogs. But the final product fits me perfectly and is comparable to a high-end custom coat. I hope to wear it for many years.

If cost is your major concern, keep an eye out for sales. You can find high-quality fabrics at incredible bargain prices, which will allow you to make show apparel for a pittance.

The best reason to sew riding apparel is that it's fun! It's immensely satisfying to use your sewing skills and creativity to produce garments that you can wear with pride.

CHAPTER 2

GETTING STARTED

Maybe by now you're thinking, "Yes, this all sounds great, but surely riding clothes must be complicated to sew?" If you have ever sewn a blouse or a pair of pants, you have all the sewing skills you need to successfully sew many items of riding apparel. You just need to be willing to invest some time and pay attention to details. Although the most challenging and time-consuming items are tailored jackets, even a less experienced sewer with no tailoring experience can produce a beautiful coat if willing to spend time and be patient.

A key to success is the willingness to experiment and tinker. The most difficult aspect of sewing riding apparel is not the sewing — it's the fitting. Proper fit is essential to correct appearance in the show ring as well as to comfort and function in the field. You must be willing to take the time to get the correct fit. For many items, I recommend making a test garment. You will also have to spend time finding and choosing the right fabrics, interfacings, and notions, considering the aesthetics of style and color, performance characteristics, or both. You also might have to try out different threads, needles, and sewing-machine adjustments for the specialized materials used for riding garments.

Before you sew a particular item of riding apparel, try to borrow the same item in ready-to-wear. Visit a tack store or a friend or trainer who has a garment you can look at. This is particularly helpful if you are not a rider yourself, but rather are an accommodating mother or grandmother who sews. If possible, look at the most expensive and high-quality garment of the type you intend to make. You probably won't be able to duplicate a ready-made garment exactly, but you can get some ideas for details and features that you can incorporate into your home-sewn garment.

Appendix II offers a list of sources for many of the types of fabrics you'll need. If you can't find the exact fabric you want, try creative substitutions. I have known people who have used all sorts of stretch fabrics for riding pants and simply adapted the pattern in clever ways. Don't necessarily try to duplicate ready-to-wear. Be flexible.

Just about every type of sewing technique is used to make riding clothes. Basic techniques are used for shirts, blouses, vests, and some riding pants. Activewear-sewing techniques, for sewing with stretch fabrics, are used to make stretch pants and tights. Leather-sewing techniques are used for making chaps and for sewing leather reinforcements onto riding breeches. To make riding outerwear, you use the same techniques required for sewing skiwear and rainwear. Finally, tailoring techniques are needed to make show jackets, such as hunt, dressage, and saddle-suit coats.

Different fabrics require different sewing techniques, different skills to obtain a good fit, and a different range of equipment. Here's a short list of specific garments you might want to sew, and the techniques, fabrics, and equipment you'll require.

BASIC RIDING APPAREL

Riding shirts, blouses, vests, and pants that are made from nonstretch fabrics all require these basic sewing skills:

✔ Sewing and finishing seams
✔ Applying sew-in and fusible interfacings
✔ Making and attaching collars, waistbands, and cuffs
✔ Sewing pockets
✔ Making buttonholes and sewing on buttons

FITTING

You'll use the same fitting methods as you would for regular apparel. Some extra steps may be required, however, for close-fitting show blouses and vests and for some riding pants, such as saddle-suit jodhpurs.

FABRICS

The best fabrics for these items are generally natural fabrics, such as cottons and cotton blends, and other woven fabrics that are easy to sew.

EQUIPMENT AND SUPPLIES

✔ You can use almost any home sewing machine that has a variable stitch length and is able to backstitch. The machine should also be able to make buttonholes. A zigzag stitch is nice to have, but not necessary.
✔ You'll also need these supplies, all of which should be available at most fabric stores:
✔ Regular sewing-machine needles in sizes suitable for your fabric. (Heavier fabrics require larger needle sizes.)

✔ A zipper foot, useful for sewing pants.
✔ Standard bent-handled sewing shears with sharp blades (either left- or right-handed).
✔ Double-pointed scissors with shorter blades than those of standard shears, useful for trimming and clipping.
✔ Good-quality measuring tape
✔ Pins in different lengths. (Long pins with round heads are good for thick and heavy fabrics.)
✔ Various types of marking pens and chalk are available. (Always test a marker before using it on your fabric.)
✔ See-through rulers and hem guides.

STRETCH GARMENTS

Breeches, jodhpurs, riding tights, and riding sweatpants made with stretch-knit and stretch-woven fabrics require activewear sewing techniques. There are special techniques for sewing elastic waistbands and leg bottoms. You'll also need to:

✔ Choose fabric with the correct weight and degree of stretch for the garment you'll be making. (The pattern and your test garment will provide some guidelines.)
✔ Find the stitch length and stitch type for the fabric. (Experiment on sample scraps of the fabric you'll be working with.)
✔ Choose the correct needle for the fabric.

FITTING

Fitting is more of an issue with stretch garments. Though stretch fabrics can be very forgiving, some trial-and-error adjustments may be needed. You'll need to take extra leg measurements and compare them to the pattern, especially for tight-fitting breeches. If you've chosen expensive breech fabric, you might want first to make a pair in a less expensive fabric to test the pattern.

FABRICS

Finding suitable stretch fabrics can be difficult. Ready-made breeches and tights use fabrics that have been custom-milled for the manufacturer. You won't find these types of fabrics in fabric stores. Suitable fabrics are out there, but you might have to do some searching or order your fabric by mail. The fabrics you're looking for are heavy-weight four-way-stretch knits, preferably nylon/spandex and cotton/spandex blends. Breeches and jodhpurs can also be made from four-way-stretch woven fabrics.

EQUIPMENT AND SUPPLIES

A common problem when sewing knit fabrics is skipped stitches. Synthetic fabrics are slippery and often have very tight weave structures. To avoid skipped stitches, you'll need to try out an assortment of sewing-machine needles — regular, ballpoint, and universal — in different sizes. This way you will be able to choose the best needle for your particular fabric.

LEATHER GARMENTS AND OTHER ITEMS

Leather chaps and leather reinforcements on riding pants protect the rider's skin from chafing. Because the stitching will leave permanent holes in the leather, you'll need to stitch accurately the first time. You'll also need to:

✔ Choose the correct type and weight of
   leather.
✔ Determine the square footage required and
   the number of hides.
✔ Lay out and cut hides into pattern pieces.
✔ Find the stitch length and stitch type for the
   leather you're working with.
✔ Choose the correct needle and thread.
✔ Use special leather-sewing techniques and
   rubber cement to "baste" seams and lock
   the ends of seams.

FITTING

Good fitting is crucial when making chaps,
especially show chaps. You must take accurate
body measurements and use them to alter the
chap pattern. I strongly recommend making a
test garment.

LEATHER

Finding and buying leather is not always
easy. If you have a good leather shop in your
area, you can take your pattern to the store
and choose the exact leather pieces that will
work best. If you can't find the leather type
and color you need locally, there are many
mail-order sources that offer a much larger
selection (see Appendix II). With mail order,
however, you will probably have to buy extra
to make sure you have enough. You are also at
the mercy of the supplier to pick out the hides.

EQUIPMENT AND SUPPLIES

The average home sewing machine can sew
most of the types of leather used for riding
apparel. Even though special sewing-machine
needles are available for sewing leather, sometimes other types of needles work better. It's a
good idea to have an assortment of needle

types on hand. You'll also need adhesive tape for attaching pattern pieces, paper clips for holding some seams together, and rubber cement to hold some pieces in place. You'll need a leather punch to install buckles and conchos (the decorative metal fasteners on chaps) as well as a rotary cutter for cutting chap fringe. You also need to know that cutting leather can really dull your shears, so consider having an extra pair that you only use for leather.

OUTERWEAR

Riding outerwear, such as dusters, outback coats, and other coats, require the same sewing methods as skiwear and general rainwear. You'll need to:

- ✔ Choose the correct type of fabric for your purpose (rain protection, warmth, etc.).
- ✔ Choose the functional features for your garment, such as snap pockets, gussets, leg straps, etc.
- ✔ Waterproof the garment by sealing the seams.
- ✔ Choose and sew an insulation material.
- ✔ Install gripper snaps (large heavy-duty fasteners crimped together with a special tool).

FITTING

Outerwear garments are easy to fit. The main concerns are the coat and sleeve lengths.

FABRICS

You'll want to use special waterproof or water-repellent fabrics, such as coated and treated nylons, Ultrex, cotton duck, etc. Some fabric stores carry these fabrics, but for the best selection consider mail-order sources. Mail-order and some retail suppliers of specialty outerwear fabrics also carry the insulations, snaps, and notions you'll need.

EQUIPMENT AND SUPPLIES

Most outerwear can be sewn with basic sewing supplies. You might find a "jeans" or "denim" sewing-machine needle helpful for sewing heavy canvas or duck dusters. I also recommend special gripper-snap setting tools, available from specialty stores and suppliers.

TAILORED COATS

Hunt coats, dressage coats, saddle-suit coats, shadbellies, and Western show jackets all require tailoring techniques. These items are the most challenging to sew, but can be successfully done if you have good basic sewing skills. You'll need to:

✔ Be patient and allow enough time. These are big projects and cannot be rushed.
✔ Know how to fit a jacket.
✔ Press correctly. (This is more important than the sewing.)
✔ Choose and apply fusible interfacing (a very large part of the job).
✔ Be precise in fitting, cutting, and sewing.
✔ Stitch neatly and evenly by hand (even for jackets made with the most modern tailoring techniques).
✔ Sew tailored collars and lapels.
✔ Make welted pockets on some coats.
✔ Set in sleeves and sew in shoulder pads.

FITTING

Fitting is a big part of making tailored coats. You have to take careful body measurements and alter the pattern pieces accordingly. You should then sew a test coat, decide if further adjustments are needed, and make these adjustments to the pattern pieces before sewing the final garment.

FABRICS

Some fabrics, interfacings, and notions are readily available at fabric stores. Sometimes the wool suiting fabrics that are appropriate for riding coats are available only seasonally. Fabrics for daycoats and Western show coats, such as heavy raw silk and metallic fabrics, can be difficult to find. Once again, try mail-order sources. Except for the beaded and sequinned fabrics often used for Western show coats, coat fabrics are generally easy to work with.

EQUIPMENT AND SUPPLIES

You'll need pinking shears to finish the inside edges of fusible interfacing pieces. For correct pressing, you'll need a good steam iron with a large, heavy soleplate. Irons that deliver a "shot" of steam are very good. To correctly fuse interfacing, you need to have both adequate heat and adequate pressure. A press cloth of a smooth fabric is mandatory when pressing the right side of the fabric. This cloth prevents the iron from scorching the coat fabric or creating a surface shine. Opinions vary as to what makes the best press cloth, but you can use a folded piece of muslin, a cotton see-through press cloth, purchased treated press cloths, or a piece of the coat fabric. Fabrics with a high synthetic content need heavier press cloths.

I also recommend several other useful pressing devices. Because purchasing all of these would add significantly to the cost of your project, I'll also suggest some substitutions.

A pressing ham is a small round stuffed cushion that is used to press shaped areas, such as darts and curved seams. As a substitute, you can fold, roll up, and firmly pin a medium-sized towel.

A seam roll is a cylindrical stuffed cushion, used to press seams open without imprinting the seam-allowance edges on the right side of the fabric. It is very useful for pressing sleeve seams, for example. Again, a simple substitute is a firmly rolled-up towel. You can also tightly roll up a magazine and cover it with a dish towel, tucking the ends of the towel into the roll ends. For a sturdier seam roll, cut a piece of dowel rod, 1/2 in. to 1 in. in diameter, to a length of 2 ft. to 3 ft. Wrap it tightly with many layers of newspaper to the desired diameter. Cover the wrapped dowel with wool knit or flannel, and securely hand-stitch the long seam and the ends to give the fabric a snug fit. I've found that a 3-ft.-long seam roll is great for pressing pants seams.

A clapper is a flat wooden block with rounded edges, which is used to flatten seams and enclosed edges, such as those at the center front of a coat. You can use a wooden ruler or other smooth piece of wood as a substitute.

A pointer is a wooden tool with a pointed end. It's used to make neat corners by pushing and rolling the stitched fabric as it's turned right side out. You can purchase various combinations of wooden clappers, pointers, and other narrow and shaped pressing surfaces.

PRESSING HAM

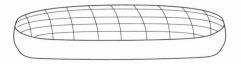

SEAM ROLL

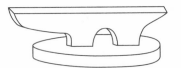

POINT PRESSER/CLAPPER

KEY TO THE DRAWINGS

In the drawings that follow, the right side of the garment (the side that will be the outer, visible side) is shaded as shown in the key below. The shading designated as "Pattern" refers to the printed side of the pattern piece. The shading designated as "Fabric" refers to the right side of the main fashion fabric used in a garment. The shading designated as "2nd Fabric" refers to a different fabric used in the same garment, such as a lining or different color fabric. The shading designated as "Interfacing or Insulation" will show one or the other in a particular set of drawings. In all cases, the wrong side of the fabric will be unshaded.

PATTERN

RIGHT
SIDE
OF FABRIC

RIGHT
SIDE
2ND FABRIC

INTERFACING
OR
INSULATION

PRESSING TECHNIQUES

Correct pressing can make the difference between a garment that looks homemade and one that looks custom-made. Pressing after the garment is finished is not enough — to produce crisp edges and corners and smooth seams and darts, you need to press often as you sew and construct the garment. Pressing is especially crucial when making tailored garments, but all of the pressing tools noted above and the following techniques are useful when making other types of garments as well.

✔ Use a good steam iron, one with a large, substantial soleplate, that produces lots of steam. If you need to protect your fabric, also use a press cloth.

✔ After sewing each seam, first press the line of stitching on the right side of the fabric. Use an up-and-down pressing motion; **do not** slide the iron — this can stretch the fabric or seam.

✔ Next open the seam and, on the wrong side of the fabric, press the seam allowances flat.

✔ Now press the seam on the right side of the fabric, being sure to use a press cloth. (The drawing does not show the press cloth.)

✔ Use a pressing ham, or substitute, for pressing darts and curved seams.

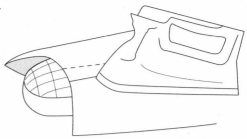

✔ Use a seam roll, or substitute, for pressing all straight seams, including sleeve seams.

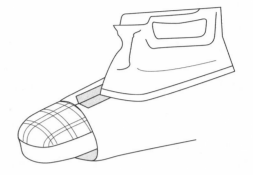

✔ Use a clapper, or substitute, for pressing enclosed seams. After pressing and steaming the seam, place the clapper on one area of the seam while the fabric is still warm. Press the clapper down firmly with both hands until the fabric is cool and dry. Repeat the process along the entire length of the seam.

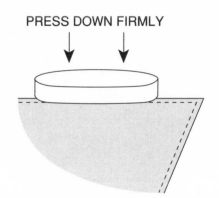

PRESS DOWN FIRMLY

REINFORCING SEAMS

Because the garments are close-fitting or subjected to vigorous body movement, or both, there's a lot of stress on the seams of riding garments. One way to reinforce seams is to double-stitch them — stitching once on the seam line of the pattern and again in the seam allowance, 1/8 in. to 1/4 in. away from the first line of stitching. The first stitching can be

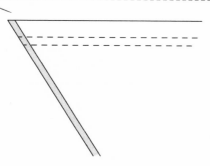
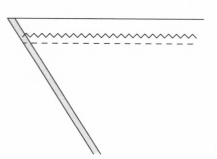

straight stitching or a very narrow zigzag stitch (barely off a straight stitch). The second stitching can be the same as the first, or a wider zigzag. I recommend double-stitching for curved seams, such as crotch seams and armhole seams.

Another way to reinforce a seam is by topstitching. After you sew the seam, press the seam allowances to one side. Then stitch on the right side of the garment, $1/8$ in. to $1/4$ in. from the seam line. This makes a good finish for straight seams because the seam allowances lie flat, and there's less bulk when you wear the garment.

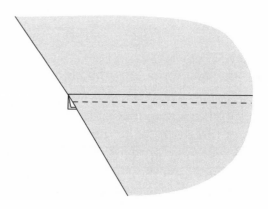

Bar-tacking is an excellent way to reinforce major stress points. To bar-tack, set your machine for a wide zigzag stitch, and set the stitch length at or near zero. Lower the needle into the fabric at the stress point and stitch back and forth in the same place for at least five or six stitches. Use bar tacks at the ends of pockets, at the bottom of fly topstitching, and at the sides of flaps and straps.

Whichever seam reinforcement you use, always start your project with a new sewing-machine needle.

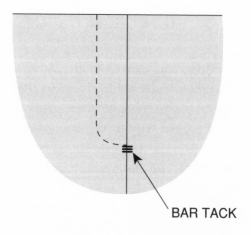

BAR TACK

CHAPTER 3

GETTING THE RIGHT FIT

As I've already mentioned, obtaining the correct fit is crucial to the success of sewing your own riding apparel. The first step toward getting a correct fit is to take accurate body measurements. Take measurements in your underwear — and don't cheat!

TAKING MEASUREMENTS AND CHOOSING PATTERN SIZE

For **jackets, vests, shirts, and blouses**, you need to take these measurements shown in the drawing:

1. Neck ....
2. Bust ....
3. Waist ....
11. Back of neck to waist ....
15. Arm length from shoulder to wrist, measuring over elbow ....

For **pants**, you need to measure:

3. Waist ....
4. High hip, above the fullest part of tummy ....
5. Hips, at the widest part ....
12. Crotch depth ....
10. Leg inseam ....

For **tight-fitting breeches and chaps** also measure:

6. Thigh diameter at crotch level ....
7. Midthigh ....
8. Knee at fullest part ....
9. Calf at fullest part ....
13. Inseam from crotch to knee ....
14. Inseam from knee to ankle ....

Compare these measurements to those given with the pattern. If no pattern measurements are given, measure the pattern pieces at the appropriate areas. Remember to allow for seam allowances and ease.

Seam allowances should be specified on the pattern and are usually 1/2 in. to 5/8 in. Ease refers to the extra fabric allowed for either comfort or fashion purposes. The extra fabric needed for comfort is called wearing ease — for example, a typical waistband is 1 in. larger than the waist measurement of the body. Wearing ease varies quite a bit, depending on the type of fit desired, the fabric, and the area of the body. Design ease is the extra fabric added for style — as, for example, in puffy sleeves — although most riding garments don't have much design ease.

If you own a garment similar to the one you're making that fits well, compare its measurements to those of the pattern. This is a very useful way to estimate sleeve, coat, and leg lengths.

Choose the pattern size based on your measurements. Pay no attention to ready-to-wear sizes. American apparel manufacturers have no sizing standards. To add to the confusion, lots of riding apparel (mostly hunt seat and dressage) is manufactured in Europe according to European sizes. Go strictly by the measurements on the pattern.

MAKING PATTERN ALTERATIONS

What if your measurements do not match the pattern's exactly? This is probably true for most people. If the pattern is multisize, you can sometimes adjust the pattern between sizes. For example, I wear a larger size above the waist than below, so I use the cutting lines for one size for the top section of a jacket and the next smaller size for the section below.

You can also simply use the largest size dictated by your measurements and take in the garment wherever needed. Another idea is to cut 1-in. seam allowances on the side, front, and back seams so that you'll have room to let out the garment where necessary. (This is especially important when working with less forgiving woven fabrics, such as wool, and when making garments for still-growing children.)

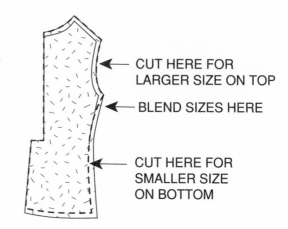

← CUT HERE FOR LARGER SIZE ON TOP

← BLEND SIZES HERE

← CUT HERE FOR SMALLER SIZE ON BOTTOM

ADJUSTING LENGTH

Before you cut out any fabric, adjust the pattern lengths for the upper torso, lower torso, sleeves, and legs. Make sure that you alter all related pieces.

The pattern measurement for the bodice of the sample riding jacket shown in the drawing is 18 in. Let's say the rider has a back-neck-to-waist measurement of 17 in. (measurement 11 in the drawing on page 20). So, we need to subtract 1 in. of the jacket's length above the waist. Measure the pattern length from the waist to the finished hem line and look at where this would put the hem of the jacket on the rider. We need an extra 1 in. of length below the waist. (Hem length is sometimes a judgment call.)

These adjustments have to be made for all the torso pieces — the front, front facing, side front, side back, and back. Don't forget to also adjust any lining or interfacing pieces.

To subtract 1 in. from the pattern piece above the waist, fold a horizontal 1/2-in. tuck between the bottom of the armhole and the waist. Redraw the cutting lines along the edges of the pattern piece, connecting them above and below the fold.

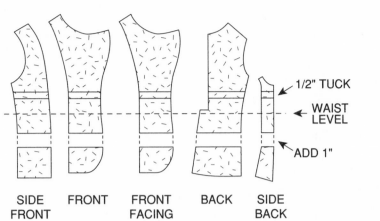

SIDE   FRONT   FRONT   BACK   SIDE
FRONT   FACING   BACK

— 1/2" TUCK

← WAIST LEVEL

ADD 1"

CLOSEUP OF 1/2" TUCK

If you only need to add 1/2 in. of length, you can often just add it at the hem. To add more, you would adjust the pattern, as for this sample jacket. To add 1 in. to the jacket pattern below the waist, cut horizontally across the pattern, midway between the waist and the hem. Tape paper to one cut edge of each pattern piece and draw a parallel line on the paper 1 in. from the cut edge. Match this line to the other cut edge. Redraw the cutting lines on the edges of the pattern pieces to blend them as needed. It is better to add needed hem length between the waist and the hem instead of at the hem because this will maintain the shape of the jacket.

ALTERING THE UPPER ARM

A common problem with fitted riding jackets and shirts is that the upper arm is too tight.

To enlarge a one-piece sleeve, measure across the pattern between the underarm seam lines as shown in the drawing. Then measure the fullest part of your upper arm. Add 1 1/2 in. to 2 in. to this measurement for ease. Subtract the sleeve-pattern measurement from this total, and divide the figure in half. Add this amount to each side of the sleeve underarm by drawing new lines. Tape extra paper to the pattern if necessary. Extend the sleeve-cap cutting line and redraw the sleeve side seams, as shown.

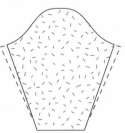

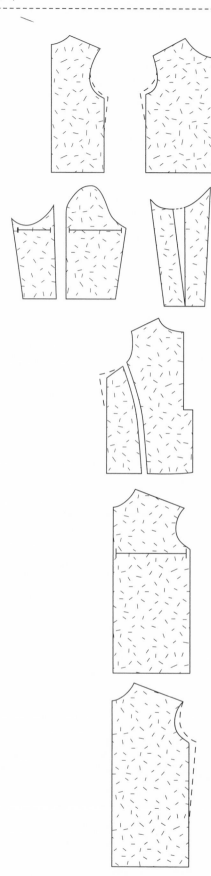

You then have to adjust the armholes of the front-side and back-side bodice pieces. Add the same total amount to each side of the bodice as you added to each side of the sleeve.

To adjust a two-part sleeve, measure across both pieces, allowing for seam allowances. Then measure the fullest part of your upper arm, and add 1 1/2 in. to 2 in. to this measurement. Subtract the sleeve-pattern measurement from this total. Slash the undersleeve piece along the underarm and add the result of your calculation at the armhole, tapering the amount to nothing at the sleeve bottom, as shown.

Then adjust the armholes of the front and back bodice pieces. Add to each underarm one half of the total you added to the sleeve.

If the garment back is two pieces, adjust the back as shown.

ALTERING FOR A BROAD BACK

Another common problem with riding jackets and shirts is that, to allow the rider free movement, there often needs to be additional width across the back at the shoulder blades.

To make this adjustment, have someone measure across your back from underarm to underarm. Add at least 1 in. of ease for shirts and 2 in. for jackets. (For back pieces with center back seams, divide measurement plus ease by 2, to determine how much to add to each half of the back.)

Next measure the pattern piece for the back in the same area in which you took your body measurement, allowing for seam allowances. Subtract the pattern measurement from the sum you computed above. Add this amount to the pattern back at the bottom of the armhole.

Redraw the armhole curve by pivoting from the end of the shoulder seam, being careful to keep the armhole curve the original length. Use the pattern as a template, and with the

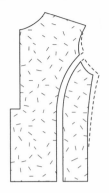

shoulder end of the shoulder seam in place, move the armhole curve out until you have the correct amount at the bottom of the armhole. Following the pattern, draw the new curve and evenly blend the seamline from the bottom of the armhole into the side seam.

The method for altering a two-piece back is similar, except that you will have to pivot the back and side back pieces as one unit. Pin the pieces together at the seam lines and then follow the method used for a one-piece back.

MAKING TEST GARMENTS

The bad news is that, before sewing riding apparel, it is often highly desirable to make a test garment. Yes, it's a nuisance and it's time-consuming, but the worst feeling in the world is trying on your finished garment and having the fit be all wrong. This is especially true if you're using an expensive fabric.

Unfortunately, it is impossible for a single pattern to fit all body types and shapes without some alteration. I strongly recommend making test garments for the following items:

✔ Tailored jackets
✔ Chaps
✔ Form-fitting Western show clothes, such as blouses and vests
✔ Stretch riding pants

To make a test garment, use a fabric similar in weight and drape to your actual garment's fabric. I find most of my test fabric on the sale table at my local fabric store for under $2 a yard. (There's more information about making specific test garments in the following chapters.)

CHAPTER 4

TAILORING COATS

Many coats worn in the show ring are tailored. Tailored riding coats include hunt coats, dressage coats, shadbellies, saddle-suit coats, daycoats, and Western show jackets. (For more detailed information about saddle-suit coats, see Chapter 8. For more information about Western show jackets, see Chapter 9.)

A tailored coat usually has a lapel, a rolled collar, two-part sleeves, and a lining. Interfacing and some special techniques are used to give the coat a crisp look and to provide extra durability, because tailored coats are usually worn many times. Hip-length coats are usually vented — that is, split at the waist in the back or side back.

HUNT COATS

The term "hunt coat" is generally used for riding jackets that are worn in hunt-seat, hunter, and jumper competitions. The coat has notched lapels, front welt pockets, three buttons in the front, and side vents in the back.

Wool and wool-blend gabardines are excellent fabrics for hunt coats. The choices for

HUNT COAT

color are dark navy (the most conservative choice), dark navy or charcoal with subtle pin-stripes, dark green, and black. The color of the lining fabric should match that of the coat fabric. Buttons should also be the same color as the fabric. Although you see hunt coats with metallic buttons, they are not correct according to current convention.

The hunt coat should fit well, but should have enough ease for needed movement. Women's coats should taper in a little at the waist. The back vents should start at or slightly below the waistline. The coat should be wide enough at the hips in back so that the vents do not gape open. The coat length should be at or slightly below crotch level, depending upon what looks best for your build. The coat must not be so long that you sit on it when in the saddle. The bottom button should be slightly above your waist. The coat back should be wide enough across the shoulders so that it doesn't pull when you bring your arms forward. The correct sleeve length allows a small amount of cuff to show when your arms are in the riding position. The sleeves should also be wide enough to give you enough room for movement. but should look trim.

DRESSAGE COATS

Dressage coats come in two styles. The first, sometimes called a frock coat, has notched lapels, a fitted waist seam, a four-button front, a center-back vent, and narrow side-back pleats. The other style, similar to a hunt coat, has four buttons, a center-back vent, and is slightly more fitted. Either style is acceptable for lower level dressage competition (as is a hunt coat), though there are regional preferences.

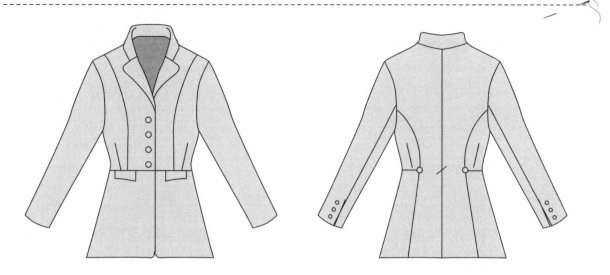

DRESSAGE COAT-FROCK STYLE

Coat and lining fabrics for dressage coats are the same as for hunt coats. The color choice is simple — dressage coats are always black or midnight blue (a very dark navy). Black is by far the most common color. You can add a little flair with black, silver, or gold buttons.

Dressage coats fit similarly to hunt coats. They are somewhat more fitted through the bodice, however. They can also be a bit longer, though should still be short enough so that you do not sit on them while in the saddle. The center-back vent should start at or slightly below your waist.

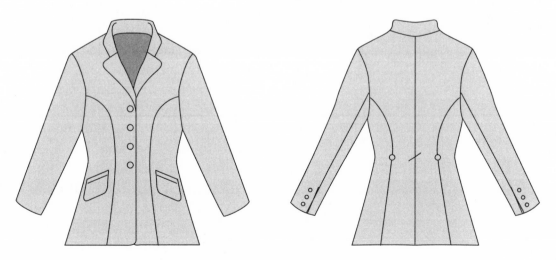

DRESSAGE COAT

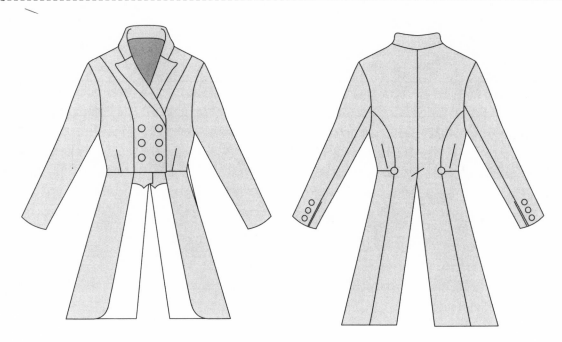

SHADBELLY COAT

SHADBELLIES

Shadbellies are formal coats with tails and are worn for higher level dressage and for some formal hunt and saddle-seat classes. They have double-breasted bodices fitted to the waist in front, with notched wing lapels. The coat is worn over a hunt vest or sometimes has fake vest points attached to the inside of the lower front of the bodice to give the appearance of a vest being worn beneath. The tails are split at center back and have side-back pleats.

Shadbellies are usually made of wool. The tails are lined with leather or water-resistant nylon to protect them from the horse's sweat. The tails are also weighted (with drapery weights, for example) so that they hang correctly. Similar to dressage coats, shadbellies are always black or very dark navy blue. The collar can be faced with satin or velvet. Buttons can be the same color as the coat — or silver or gold. The vest points are always canary yellow.

The shadbelly bodice should be form-fitting, but should allow enough ease through the back and shoulders for a smooth fit. The sleeves should be long enough so that they hit the wristbone when the rider's arms are in the riding position. The tails should lie neatly behind the rider, with their hems hanging at the same level as the rider's knee. When the rider is standing, the hem length of the tails will be at or slightly above the back of the knees.

FABRICS AND NOTIONS

For many riding coats, the best fabric to use is a wool gabardine. Gabardine is a twill fabric, with a fine, diagonal weave. You can use wool-blend or synthetic gabardines if your budget is tight, but buy the best quality you can afford. Synthetic fabrics do not shape as nicely as wool and do not "breathe."

The quality of the lining fabric should match the quality of the coat fabric, but be lighter in weight and softer. Medium-weight nylon or polyester linings are good choices. Rayon or rayon/acetate linings are more comfortable to wear in hot weather, but are not as durable. Shrinkage can also be a problem, especially for saddle-suit coats, which are subjected to the horse's body heat.

The most expensive tailored coats are hand-tailored. Hair-canvas interfacing is hand-sewn into the coat with a variety of special stitches. The coat is shaped by hand as it is being stitched. It is a **very** time-consuming method, takes some practice to do well, and I do not recommend it.

I recommend fusible interfacing and machine-stitching wherever possible. Fusible interfacing has a resin coating on one side, which fuses to the fabric when activated with the heat of an iron. You must use the right interfacing for your fabric, but if you do, this

method is the fastest and easiest way to tailor
and produces a very nice result.

The **only** way to choose the correct fusible
interfacing is to test several different types by
fusing them to a sample piece of your coat fabric. I cannot emphasize enough how important
this is.

Woven, nonwoven, and weft-insertion types
of fusible interfacing are all suitable for riding
coats. Opinions vary as to which are best.
Some are designated specifically for tailoring,
and these are good to try. I have had good
luck with woven and weft-insertion interfacing.
With so many different types and weights of
fusible interfacing available, you should be
able to find the one that will be just right for
your riding-coat fabric. The most important
consideration is that the interfacing should
match the weight of the fabric. Keep in mind
that riding coats should look smooth and crisp,
so stay away from the softer, more flexible
interfacings.

Buy small quantities of several different
types of fusible interfacing that seem suitable
for the weight of your coat fabric. (For most
riding coats, this will be a medium-weight
interfacing.) Cut small squares of each type of
interfacing and pink one edge of each. Fuse
the squares to the wrong side of the sample
piece of fabric, according to the manufacturer's
instructions. Check the following:

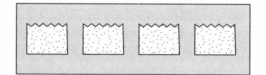

1. Are the pinked or straight edges of the
    interfacing visible from the right side of the
    fabric? If so, the interfacing is too heavy.

2. Try to pull off the interfacing. If you suc-
    ceed, it is not securely bonded to the fab-
    ric. Try fusing again, increasing the temper-
    ature, pressure, or length of time. Also
    check that the fabric is smooth and without
    puckers.

3. After you have fused the interfacing, drape
    the sample piece of fabric over your hand
    and try folding it to simulate layers of fabric

in the garment. Does it drape and hang nicely? Do the layers feel good together? Does it have a smooth appearance?

MAKING A TEST COAT

Yes, it is a royal pain to cut out and sew a test garment, **but** it is the only way to really get a good fit. Riding coats are fairly form-fitting. Other methods of fitting, such as pinning pattern pieces together, just aren't adequate.

You should make your test coat from an inexpensive fabric substantial enough to hang correctly. Check the clearance table at your fabric store for cotton-blend sportswear fabrics.

Cut out the front, back, sleeve, and upper collar pieces. You can add 1-in. seam allowances to the shoulder and all vertical seams if you think you might need to let out the coat in places. You do not need front facing, an undercollar, or any pocket pieces. Mark the coat roll line, the center fronts, waistline, the sleeve lengthwise-grain lines, and any pocket positions on the right side of the fabric.

Sew the bodice of the coat together, and add the sleeves and collar. Press open all seam allowances. Press under seam allowances on the center-front edges of the coat and on the collar, and stitch around these edges. Press the lapels open at the roll lines. Pin the back vents, if any, in place, and pin the sleeve and coat hems — with pins on the outside of the garment. Also pin the shoulder pads in place.

Now try the coat on over your riding shirt and vest, if you wear one. (I even put on my riding breeches for this step.)

Pin the front of the coat together, matching the center fronts. Also insert pins at the buttonhole locations. Check the general fit, as well as back-neck-to-waist length, sleeve length, back

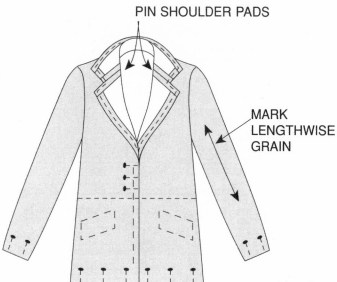

PIN SHOULDER PADS

MARK
LENGTHWISE
GRAIN

width, sleeve width, coat length, and lapel width. Remember that the finished coat will be lined, so the test garment should feel a tad large. Check how the sleeves hang and how they look with a bent arm. The sleeve length-wise-grain line should be straight. Check the button and pocket positions, if any. The lapels should not gape, and the collar should lie smoothly around the neckline. Also check where the back vents start and whether or not they hang correctly (gaping back vents are not attractive). The vents should start at or slightly below the waist.

After checking out the test garment at home, take it with you the next time you ride and try it out in the saddle. Is it comfortable to wear? Is the length correct for your riding disci-pline? (I had a hand-me-down dressage coat that drove me nuts in training-level tests because it was too long. I would sit on the back hem during every rising trot sequence.) Also make sure that the sleeves hang correctly and are the correct length when you're holding the reins, as discussed above.

If you have to make major changes, such as a size change or alterations of more than an inch or two, you should sew another test coat. Otherwise, note any adjustments you'd like to make and alter your pattern pieces accordingly.

Remember, the most important thing you can do to sew a nice riding coat is to press correctly! A riding coat is a structured, fairly form-fitting garment and must have a crisp, smooth appearance in the show ring. Step-by-step pressing is necessary to produce this shaped, smooth look. Review the section on pressing in Chapter 2, and press after each step of sewing your coat.

LAPELS

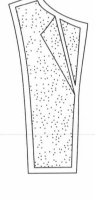

A nicely rolled lapel is important to the look of your riding coat. Twill tape, available at fabric stores, is used to reinforce the lapel fold and to pull the lapel into the correct position. To make a nice lapel, cut an extra piece of interfacing for the lapel, using the roll line on the front pattern piece as a guide. Fuse this piece to the lapel before fusing the front interfacing.

Measure the length of the roll line from seam line to seam line. Subtract 1/4 in. for a small bust, 3/8 in. for a medium bust, and 1/2 in. for a large bust. Cut 1/4-in.-wide twill tape to this length for each lapel.

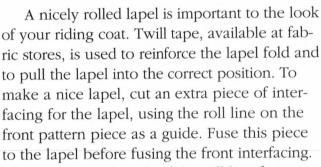

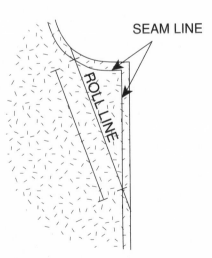

SEAM LINE

ROLL LINE

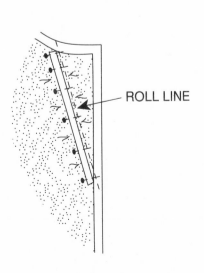

ROLL LINE

Pin the twill tape to the inside of the roll line. The ends of the tape should be pinned securely where they meet the seam lines. Ease the coat fabric under the tape along the roll line, pinning frequently. The shortened tape will pull the lapel into the correct position.

Sew down each tape with a wide zigzag stitch (12 stitches per inch). This stitching will be concealed when the lapels roll back.

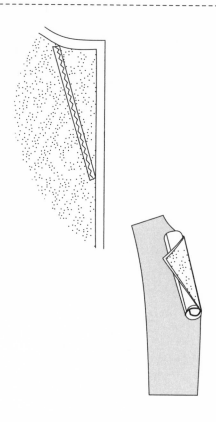

Roll up a small towel and steam each lapel in the correct shape. Let the fabric cool and dry. Even though you'll be working more with these pieces, the lapels will maintain their shape even when the coat is done!

COLLARS

Many riding coats have the same type of collar that is used for men's suit coats. The upper collar is cut from the coat fabric. The undercollar is not made from the coat fabric, but rather from a nonwoven heavy substance. I recommend Ultrasuede. Match the color of the undercollar material as closely as possible to the coat color.

Cut interfacing for the undercollar pieces and fuse them to the Ultrasuede pieces. (Use the same interfacing as you used for the coat.) Sew the center back seam of the undercollar and press the seam allowances open. Now cut a piece of interfacing to fit the stand area and fuse that piece on top of the center back seam.

Pin the undercollar to the pressing ham (or a substitute) in the same shape it will be when

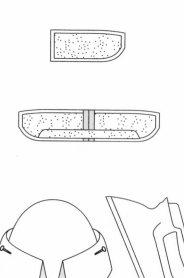

attached to the garment. Steam the undercollar
to set the shape. Let it cool and dry completely.

Your pattern pieces probably had dots on
the neck edges of the front pieces to designate
the collar ends. Staystitch between these
points, and then, every inch or so, clip the fabric to the row of staystitching.

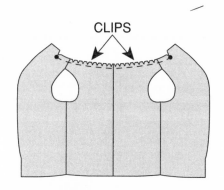

Pin the undercollar to the top of the neck
edge between the dots. Because the undercollar has no seam allowance, it will overlap the
neck edge by the width of the seam allowance.
Match any pattern markings on the undercollar
to those on the coat. With a wide zigzag (12
stitches per inch), stitch over the undercollar
edge, as shown in the drawing.

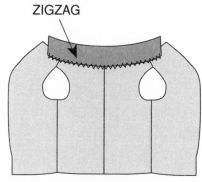

The pattern instructions will tell you to sew
the upper collar to the neck edges of the front
facings. Then sew the front facings to the coat.
The upper collar remains free.

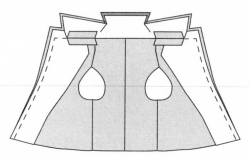

Fold under the seam allowances of the
upper collar and press.

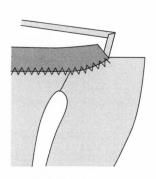

Pin the two collars together so that the
upper collar is slightly larger than the undercollar. Make sure everything is neat and symmetri-
cal. Slipstitch the two collar edges together
with stitches that are as invisible as possible.

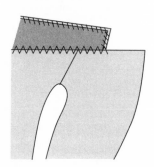

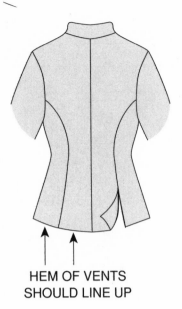

HEM OF VENTS
SHOULD LINE UP

BACK VENTS

Back vents that hang correctly are also essential to an elegant coat. When hemming the coat and finishing the vent or vents, check and double-check that the vents line up correctly, as shown in the drawing.

CARE AND CLEANING

Horses always seem to rub their runny noses on you when you're wearing your tailored coat, so it's a challenge to keep your coat clean. After each show, brush off as much dirt and hair as possible. Remove spots with a barely damp sponge, and gently lift stubborn hairs with cellophane or masking tape. Press the coat if you need to, but do not press dirt spots.

At the end of the season, have your coat dry-cleaned. If your coat has anything other than plain plastic buttons, either remove them or cover them with foil before dry-cleaning. The less frequently you dry-clean your coat, the longer it will last.

Don't store a coat in plastic—wrap it in old sheeting or use a fabric garment bag so that the coat fabric can breathe. Hang it on a padded hanger so that it retains its shape.

CHAPTER 5

RIDING PANTS

Riding pants, which include breeches, jodhpurs, tights, and sweatpants, differ from regular pants in that they are designed to fit correctly while you're riding. The construction of riding pants is not too different from that of regular pants. but there are special fitting considerations that must be considered while you're sewing.

TYPES OF RIDING PANTS

Breeches are worn by hunt, dressage, and event riders. They are worn with tall dress or field boots, have knee or leg reinforcement patches, and the legs end above the ankles.

In recent years, manufacturers have come out with a wide range of breech styles. The most common style seen in the show ring is the stretch breech. This very close-fitting style has a front or side zipper. Most have no inseam and the side seam curves to the front of the leg for riding comfort. Hunt jodhpurs are similar, but are full length with cuffed bottoms and are worn with paddock boots. Full-seat breeches, worn by dressage riders, have a leather insert along the inside of the legs to the seat. (Saddle-suit jodhpurs are a totally different style, as discussed in Chapter 8.)

Styles range from semi-fitted pants with pleated fronts to the old cavalry-type flared breeches made from nonstretch fabrics. Most can also be made as jodhpurs. Show riders usually wear fitted stretch breeches, though a small but growing number of riders are wearing pleated front pants.

The newest styles on the riding-pants scene are riding tights and sweatpants. The riding versions of these activewear favorites usually feature knee reinforcements and no inseams.

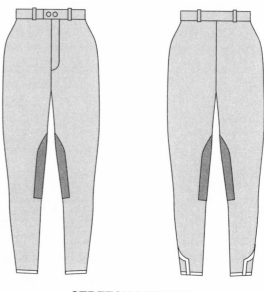

STRETCH BREECH

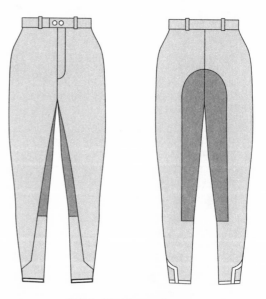

FULL SEAT BREECH

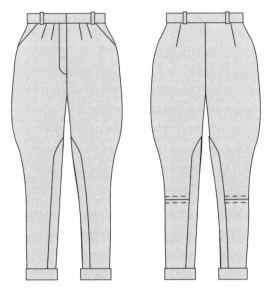

FLARED JODHPURS

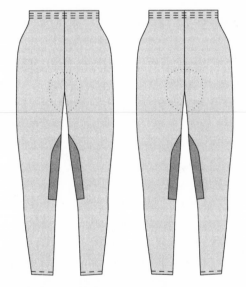

RIDING TIGHTS

Riding tights are also available with the same kind of crotch padding found in bicycle shorts or with full seat reinforcements. Riding sweatpants are more form-fitting than regular sweatpants, but looser than breeches and tights.

Manufacturers are now also coming out with riding pants that are hybrids of breeches and tights. So almost any combination of styles can be had. Home sewers have been creating their own variations for years, and you can too.

FABRICS

One of the questions I hear most often is: "Where can I buy breech fabric?" Breech manufacturers have their fabric custom-milled, and it is not usually available to the home sewer. Thanks to the growing interest in sewing activewear, however, many acceptable fabrics can be found at fabric stores. For close-fitting riding pants, you want to use four-way-stretch fabrics, which stretch both lengthwise and crosswise. The best fabric for stretch breeches and jodhpurs are heavy-weight knits with a spandex content of 2 percent to 10 percent. (Spandex is the generic name for Lycra and similar fibers.) Stretch wovens with spandex are also available. Many spandex-blend fabrics are produced in Europe, so a fabric store that carries imported fabrics is a good potential source. If you can't locate these fabrics, heavy-weight polyester and nylon doubleknits also make inexpensive, durable pants. Look for doubleknits without shiny or slippery surfaces.

Another possibility for cold-weather riding is stretch-ski-pant fabric, which comes in different wool/synthetic blends and is fairly heavy in weight. Make sure the ski-pant fabric has four-way stretch. Some types of this fabric have lengthwise stretch, but no crosswise stretch,

and this will not work for riding breeches!
Sometimes, even the four-way-stretch ski-pant
fabric does not have enough stretch for very
close-fitting breech styles. All breech fabrics
should have both crosswise and lengthwise
stretch. A crosswise stretch of at least 30 percent is recommended (this means that 10 in. of
fabric will stretch to 13 in.).

Nonstretch breeches and jodhpurs are really
fun because you can make them from many
different fabrics. The classic choice is a cotton
twill, but consider other cottons and cotton-
blends, denim, corduroy, wools, and wool
blends. You can make cotton versions for hot
weather and corduroy or wool pants for cold
weather.

Riding tights can be made from spandex,
nylon-spandex, and cotton-spandex blends.
Your options at fabric stores are usually the
swimwear and aerobicwear fabrics. The stretch
of these fabrics can vary from 50 percent to 100
percent crosswise and lengthwise, so once
again, you might have to do some trial-and-error
fitting. Some mail-order companies specialize in
these types of fabrics (see Appendix II).

Riding sweatpants are made from sweatshirt
fleece, preferably of a heavier weight, which
can be harder to find. A wonderful option is
polyester bunting such as Polarfleece or
Polarplus. This very warm and comfortable fabric dries quickly. It is also very easy to sew and
does not ravel, so you don't need to finish fabric edges. You can also use heavier weight cotton knits for hot-weather pants.

LEATHER AND SUEDE PATCHES

Riding pants need knee and leg reinforcements for added protection at these friction
points and to minimize slipping. The most
common type of reinforcements are knee
patches on the inseam of the pants. A variation
of this is the leg patch, which extends all the

way up the inner thigh. Dressage riders like full-seat breeches with leather inserts in the seat and inner-leg areas.

You can make knee patches from the pants fabric. This option is inexpensive and convenient, and the pants can be washed without special considerations. The disadvantage is that fabric knee patches wear out faster than leather ones and have no gripping ability. Self-fabric knee patches are best for riding pants made from lightweight or inexpensive fabrics.

Suede-leather knee patches are long wearing, give better protection than fabric patches, and do not slip. Suede can be difficult to find, however, especially in the correct color, and adds to the expense of the garment. Riding pants with real leather patches also require special care in washing, and the patches will eventually dry out and crack.

Use real leather with heavy-weight fabrics and when you want the protection and grip the material gives you. Real leather is the first choice for full-seat inserts because dressage riders want to be "stuck" to the saddle.

The best and most easily found material for knee patches is 2 oz. to 3 oz. chap-split cowhide suede. Full-seat inserts can also be made from smooth leather in a similar weight. Cowhide or deerskin can also be used. Deerskin is very soft and washes up nicely, but can be more difficult to sew than cowhide because of skipped stitches. If you find you have this problem, try different needle types (universal, ball point, and regular) and be sure to use a good-quality nylon or polyester thread. (See Chapter 7 for more information on buying and sewing real leather.)

Riding-apparel manufacturers use a variety of synthetic materials for knee patches and seat inserts that are not available to the public, but you can buy synthetic suede such as Ultrasuede and synthetic leather such as Ultraleather. Although these fabrics are expensive and don't provide as much protection and grip as real leather does, they are easy to sew and are available in many colors. Both synthetic materials can be machine-washed and dried and are long wearing. Consider using them for riding tights and sweatpants, whose fabrics are usually too lightweight for real leather. And it's nice to be able to throw riding sweatpants in the dryer. Use the heaviest weight possible to get the best protection.

NOTIONS

The standard polyester coil zipper works well for all types of riding pants. For pockets with visible zippers, you can sometimes find zippers with decorative pulls.

Ready-made breeches and jodhpurs are usually fastened at the waistband with 1/2-in. snaps, which are sold in fabric stores along with little tools with which to attach them. These snaps nicely duplicate the look of ready-made breeches, but they can be difficult to install, especially in heavy-weight knit breech fabrics. They also eventually pop out of the fabric. If you make a lot of breeches or other garments that use snaps (such as duster-style coats), consider buying a better tool to apply gripper snaps (see Chapter 10). You can also sew on buttons or hooks and eyes.

Breech bottoms are usually fastened using hook-and-loop tape, sold by the inch at fabric stores.

FITTING PANTS

Even though stretch breeches and jodhpurs are made with forgiving fabrics, obtaining a good fit can take some work. The fit will depend upon the amount of stretch in the fabric. If you are using an expensive fabric, I recommend first making a test pair in a less expensive fabric, such as a doubleknit.

One complication, however, is that the test-garment fabric will probably not have the same stretch qualities as the more expensive fabric, but you'll be able to get a fairly good idea of how the pattern works. If at all possible, try to find a test fabric that has the same amount of stretch as the garment fabric. Working with a very stretchy fabric, you may sew a leg one size smaller than you would if you were working with a less stretchy fabric. Unfortunately sometimes the only way to figure this out is to sew a pair.

Before you cut out the fabric, check the crotch depth and inseam length of the pattern pieces. The crotch depth for the pants should be the same as the crotch-depth body measurement (taken from the waist down while you're in a seated position). The legs of a pair of breeches should end several inches above the anklebones. For jodhpurs, the leg should end at the instep of the boot.

If you have to lengthen and shorten the pants significantly, you should do it both above and below the knee. Compare the crotch-to-knee and knee-to-hem pattern measurements with the body measurements, and add or subtract length accordingly. If you are making breeches without inseams and with a side seam that curves around the knee, the side edges can become very discontinuous. Just smooth out the cutting lines as best as you can, and they should match up just fine.

If you are using very stretchy fabric and want very snug pants, another thing to check is leg circumference. Measure your leg at midthigh and at the largest part of the calf. Compare this to the pattern measurements in the same places, remembering to allow for

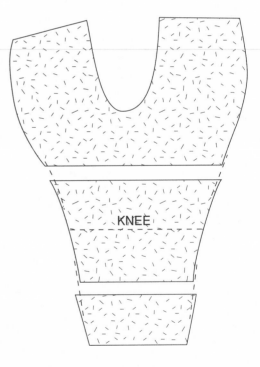

seam allowances. For stretchy fabrics, the pants should measure the same or 1 in. less than the body measurements. If you need to make the pants leg smaller or larger, either adjust the pattern between sizes or subtract or add to the side seams equally. For example, if your pants have only side seams and no inseams and you need to subtract 1 in. from each leg, subtract 1/2 in. from the front side seam and 1/2 in. from the back side seam, blending the edges of the cutting line into the hip area.

You can also take in side seams while making the pants. If you are making the pants style with the seam that curves around the knee, you might run into problems if you have to take in the seam very much. You have to sew on the knee patches first, and they could end up in the wrong position. So try and adjust the leg circumference as much as possible before cutting out the pattern pieces.

Once you've made your first pair of pants, don't judge the fit until you ride in them.

SEWING STRETCH FABRICS

Stretch fabrics have a reputation of being difficult to sew. This is because some stretch fabrics are prone to skipped stitches (for example, those fabrics used for riding tights). To minimize the possibility of skipped stitches, pre-wash the fabric with laundry soap. Use a new universal needle or a needle intended for knits. Try different sizes if the first one doesn't work.

You don't need a fancy machine with the latest stretch stitches to sew knit fabrics. As a matter of fact, a custom-breech maker I know started out using stretch stitches, but switched to regular straight and zigzag stitches because the stretch stitches seemed to be causing "runs" in the fabric. Although I have also talked to people who have used stretch stitches successfully. Once again, you need to experiment to find which of your sewing machine's stitches work best for the fabric you are using.

To sew stretch knits, use a straight stitch or a very narrow zigzag that is barely off a straight stitch. I use 12 stitches per inch for most breech fabrics. For spandex riding-tight fabric, I use a longer stitch, perhaps 8 or 9 stitches per inch. Stretch the fabric slightly both behind and in front of the needle as you sew. Finish the seam by stitching again in the seam allowance, $1/8$ in. from the first line of stitching. For breech and riding-tight seams, I sew two rows of stitching as described above, and then I either add a row of medium-width zigzag stitching in the seam allowance or I topstitch the seam with both seam allowances under the topstitching. (I started doing this after several frustrating experiences with popped seams.)

SEWING KNEE PATCHES

When sewing knee patches to pants or tights that don't have inseams, it's a good idea to check the position of the patches before sewing. They should be positioned on the insides of the legs, with each patch vertically centered at the knee.

If you are using fabric or synthetic-suede knee patches, pin them in place to check them. If you're using leather, test the position before pinning the patches so that you put as few holes as possible in the leather. You can either cut sample fabric patches and pin these to the pants, or mark the knee-patch position with a disappearing marker or chalk (check the marker or chalk on a fabric scrap first to make sure you can remove the marks). Hold the garment up to your leg to check the patch position. The placement for breeches with a side seam that curves over the knee can be a little tricky, especially if you alter the leg. If in doubt, pin or baste the side seam and try on the pants to double-check the patch position.

Once you've found the correct patch positions, you can sew them on. (If you're using leather patches, see Chapter 7 for tips on sewing leather. Remember, try to use as few pins as possible on leather.) I use the same needle for sewing the patches that I use for the garment, but you might have to experiment with different needle types and sizes. Practice on scraps first. Sew the outside edge of the patch first with a large zigzag stitch. Backstitch with a straight stitch directly below the lower edge of the patch, and then stitch forward with the zigzag. (This locks the stitching more securely than backstitching with the zigzag.)

When sewing any type of patch to stretch fabrics, slightly stretch the fabric out from under the patch as you sew around it. For very stretchy fabrics, stretch the fabric a little more. This prevents the fabric from bunching up under the patch.

Add a second row of stitching 1/2 in. inside the first. This row can be a narrow or wide zigzag stitch or a long straight stitch. Self-fabric patches look nice with additional stitching as shown in the drawing. The extra stitching stabilizes the patch. Leather patches do not need to be stabilized, and synthetic suede can be treated either way.

FINISHING LEG BOTTOMS

Breech bottoms used to have zippers, but now most have hook-and-loop tapes. The leg closure is made simply by overlapping seams or an extended tab. The tabs are nice because they give a more secure fit.

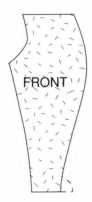

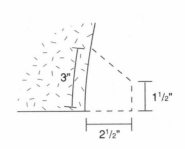

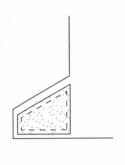

ADDING A TAB

If your pattern doesn't have a tab closure, it's easy to add one. Add a tab extension of approximately 2 1/2 in. to the front of the pants-leg bottom, as shown in the drawing. (Please note that this can affect the yardage requirement.)

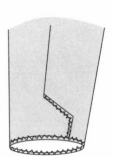

Interface the tab with sew-in interfacing, because it will be subjected to a lot of stress. The leg bottom, including the tab, can be finished with a double-fold seam binding. The hook-and-loop tape closure is attached to the tab.

ELASTICIZED LEG BOTTOMS

Elasticized leg bottoms are popular for tights and for the new breech/tight hybrids. You can also convert stretch-breech leg bottoms with hook-and-loop tape closures to elasticized bottoms. Use knitted or woven elastic for the best results.

Add length to the leg bottom if necessary so that the leg ends 1 in. to 2 in. above the ankle. Sew the side seams and inseams (if any).

Now measure the diameter of the finished edge of the leg bottom. To determine the length of elastic you'll need, for adult sizes, subtract 2 in. from this measurement; for children's sizes, subtract 1 in. Cut two pieces of 3/8-in. elastic to the length required.

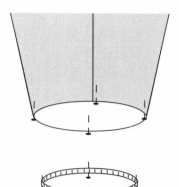

Butt the ends of each elastic piece, and stitch across them securely with a wide zigzag and a short stitch length.

Divide each leg bottom and each elastic into fourths and mark the intervals with pins. Pin the elastic to the **wrong sides** of each leg bottom, making sure the elastic is even with bottom edge of the pants leg.

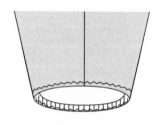

Stitching on the **elastic**, zigzag close to the edges of the leg bottoms with a narrow stitch, stretching the elastic as you sew.

Fold the elastic to the wrong side of the leg bottoms and pin it in place. With 8 stitches per inch, topstitch 1/4 in. from the folded edges, stretching the fabric as you sew.

ZIPPERED POCKETS

A zippered pocket is a nice feature to have in riding pants. Use the pattern in Appendix III to add a zippered pocket to the front of your breeches.

For each pocket, you'll need: a 7-in. zipper, 1/4-yd. of cotton fabric, a 2-in x 6-in. piece of sew-in interfacing.

Before doing anything else, cut two pocket pieces. Mark the zipper-opening box on the **wrong side** of one of the pieces. (The drawings show the pocket on the left-hand side of the pants, but you can add a pocket on either side or on both sides.)

Place the pocket piece on the front of the pants to determine its position. Mark the position of the zipper opening. The zipper opening should slant down to the side of the pants.

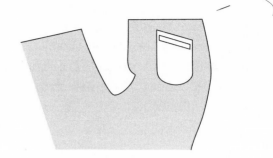

Pin the piece of interfacing to the **wrong side** of the pants, under the zipper opening.

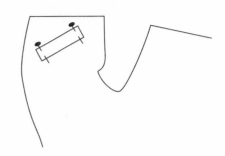

Pin the pocket to the pants front, with right sides together, matching the zipper-opening markings on the pieces. Start at the middle of the rectangle, stitch around the zipper-opening box with small straight stitches. Slash the fabric between the rows of stitching, cutting diagonally to the corners as shown in the drawing. Turn the pocket to the wrong side of the pants, and press.

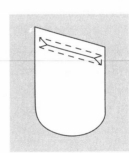

Place the zipper under the opening and pin it in place. (For thick fabrics, such as heavyweight stretch nylon, hand-baste the zipper in place.) The zipper pull will be at the upper end of the opening when the zipper's closed. The end of the zipper will extend past the opening. Topstitch close to the edges of the zipper opening and remove the basting stitches, if any.

Pin the remaining pocket piece to the pocket on the pants. Stitch around all the edges, catching the triangles of fabric at the ends of the zipper. Zigzag-stitch around the seam allowances.

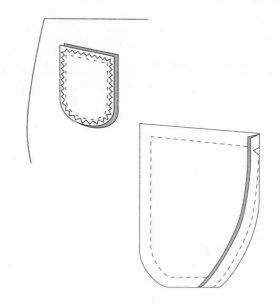

CONVERTING A COMMERCIAL PATTERN

You can convert a commercial pants pattern into riding breeches or into the currently fashionable, older style of jodhpurs made of non-stretch fabric. Choose a pattern suitable for woven fabrics, with flare through the hips and thighs and a narrow lower leg. (Some commercial patterns already have knee patches. If not, use the knee-patch pattern in Appendix III.)

For each pair of knee patches, you'll need 1 sq. ft. of suede or another suitable material. Cut two knee patches, being sure to flop the pattern and cut two opposite shapes if using leather.

If you're making breeches, determine your desired inseam length. For the average man or woman, it should be around 4 in. above your ankle bone (children's lengths vary). Cut the bottoms of the pants front and back pattern pieces to this length.

If you're making jodhpurs with cuffs, you'll need 4 1/2 in. of length below the finished hemline.

Sew the pants according to the pattern instructions, but sew the inseams and attach the knee patches before sewing the side seams.

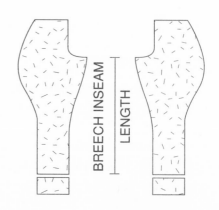

For breeches, taper in the side and inseams so that the pants bottoms are 1¹/₂ in. to 2 in. larger than the measurement of your leg at that point.

Add a tab extension to the leg bottoms, if desired, enclose the raw edges in double-fold bias tape, and sew on the hook-and-loop tapes, as described on page 49.

CARE AND CLEANING

Riding pants made from any fabric containing spandex should not be machine-dried. Exposure to heat will cause the fabric to wear out faster.

Riding pants with real leather patches or inserts should be washed in cool water with a nondetergent soap and line-dried. I've tried Murphy's Oil Soap, which works nicely if you don't mind the distinctive smell. If your pants are really dirty, you can use warm water, but try not to do this too often. The less you wash leather, the longer it will last. After it dries, the leather will probably be stiff. You can rub it with your hand to soften it; it will also soften as you wear the pants.

For riding pants made from other fabrics, simply follow the care instructions appropriate for the fabric.

CHAPTER 6

RIDING SHIRTS

Types of riding shirts include the ratcatcher shirt, Western shirt, tuxedo shirt, and Western show blouses. Many riding shirts are similar in basic design to the standard dress shirt. Shirts with shirt tails are often longer in the back in order to stay neatly tucked in while you're riding. Shirts and blouses worn for Western show classes are extremely fitted and are often made as bodysuits for a very sleek look. Zippers either in the front or the back eliminate gaping.

FABRICS AND NOTIONS

Many types of riding shirts can be made from good-quality cottons and cotton blends — broadcloth or oxford cloth are good choices. With these fabrics, a medium-weight, woven, sew-in interfacing creates a nice crisp look. Heavier interfacing can be used for collars and cuffs than for the front buttoned edges.

FITTING

The sleeve length is very important for a riding shirt. When worn under a tailored coat, the shirt sleeve should be long enough so just a hint of the cuff is visible when your arms are in the riding position. So if you are making both a coat and a shirt, make the coat first.

Make sure that the shirt is long enough in back to stay tucked in while riding. Also check the fit through your torso. Allow enough room to move comfortably, but keep a trim look. You can add darts in the front and back or make existing darts wider to give your shirt a little more fit.

ALTERING THE SHIRT COLLAR

A common problem is a shirt neck that is too tight for comfort or too loose for a nice fitted appearance. There are several ways to adjust the fit of the neck.

Choose the shirt size that fits your torso. Then measure the collar-pattern piece at the neck edge from center front to center front. Compare this to your neck measurement. The collar should be 1 in. to 1 1/2 in. larger than your neck. If your pattern is multisize, you can use a larger or smaller size of collar and neck edge, and blend the pattern lines into the body of the shirt.

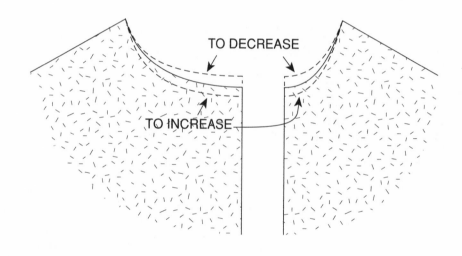

TO DECREASE

TO INCREASE

If your pattern is not multisize, there are two ways to adjust the neck. One way is to redraw the neck-edge curve — making it lower to increase the neck size and higher to decrease it. A change of only 1/8 in. can change the collar size by as much as 1/2 in. Copy the curve, using a flexible ruler if you have one. Then measure the seamline by placing a tape measure on its edge. Remember to account for shoulder seam allowances. Alter the collar piece at the center back and also between the center front and the shoulder-seam dots.

ALTER AT DASHED LINES

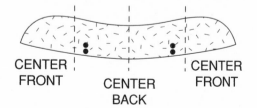

CENTER FRONT   CENTER BACK   CENTER FRONT

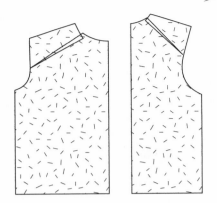

TO INCREASE NECK SIZE   TO DECREASE NECK SIZE

An alternative method of adjusting neck fit is to slash the shirt-front pattern piece from the middle of the neckline to the armhole. Then pivot the upper section at the armhole, spreading the two sections apart to increase or overlapping to decrease the neck size. Measure the neck-edge seamline and alter the collar as described above.

TYPES OF RIDING SHIRTS

The ratcatcher is the traditional shirt worn for fox hunting. It is similar to a standard dress shirt except for the stand-up collar. The shirt is semi-fitted to allow the rider movement for jumping and posting. A choker, a separate wide collar band, is worn over the collar when the shirt is worn with a hunt coat. A stock tie is worn with dressage coats and shadbellies. A stock tie is a very long tie, narrower in the middle than at the ends, which is wrapped once around the neck and tied in front with a square knot; the ends are tucked into the front of the coat.

Cotton and cotton-blend fabrics (again, broadcloth or oxford cloth) are good choices for these shirts. White shirts are always correct.

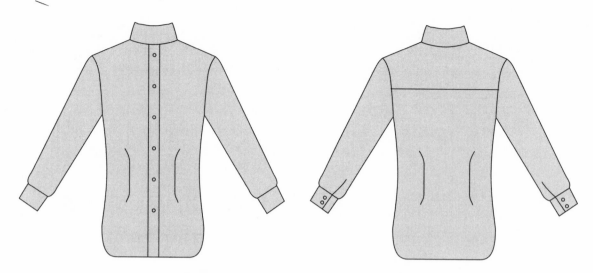

RATCATCHER SHIRT WITH CHOKER

Pale pastels in solids or stripes or white-on-white stripes are also worn in hunter classes.

Western shirts are also similar to standard dress shirts, with the addition of peaked Western yokes on the front and back and sometimes of front buttoned pockets. Many style variations exist. The shirt is semi-fitted for a trim look and is usually worn by men in Western performance classes. These shirts can be made from cotton and cotton blends in solid colors, stripes, plaids, and prints. The traditional Western shirt has pearl snaps instead of

WESTERN SHIRT WITH PEAKED YOKES

buttons. A newer variation that is very popular is the caped yoke shirt. The yoke, which is usually longer than traditional yokes, is sewn into the shoulder seams, but hangs separately from the shirt. The yoke peaks are buttoned to the shirt.

In recent years, the variety of styles, colors, and fabrics of the women's blouses seen in Western pleasure classes has increased dramatically. Western yokes, ruffles, and lace have given way to sleek designs. Ultrasuede, sequins, beaded fabrics, and gold lamé are all used. The common denominator is a very form-fitting look. Bodysuit versions are popular. (These blouses are discussed in more detail in Chapter 9.)

Tuxedo shirts for show apparel are identical in style to traditional tuxedo shirts with pin-tucked fronts. They are worn in Western show classes and formal saddle-seat classes. For Western show classes, these shirts are often made in brilliant colors or are hand-painted with striking designs.

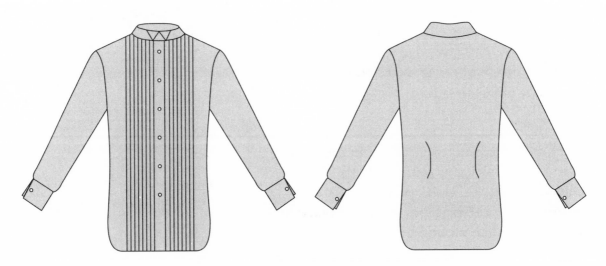

TUXEDO SHIRT

SEWING A CHOKER

The choker of a ratcatcher shirt will often wear out before the shirt does, so the more expensive shirts that you buy come with two chokers. If you need a new choker for your shirt (and can find fabric that matches), use the choker pattern in Appendix III. This pattern will fit the average-sized woman. For smaller or larger women, men, or children, hold the pattern around the wearer's neck and add or subtract length at the center front if needed.

You'll need 1/4 yd. each of choker fabric and medium-weight woven interfacing and a 1-in. length of 3/4-in.-wide hook-and-loop tape.

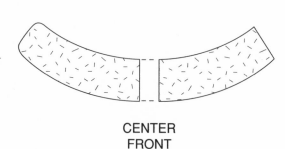

CENTER FRONT

Cut **two** choker pieces from the fabric and **one** from the interfacing. Pin the interfacing to the **wrong side** of one choker piece. This unit will be the choker facing. Cut diagonally across the corners on the straight end, as shown in the drawing. Machine-baste the interfacing to the choker, 3/8 in. from the edges.

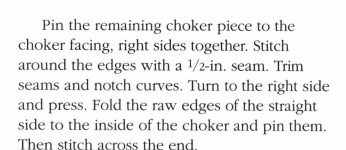

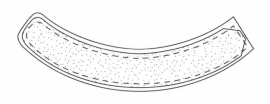

Pin the remaining choker piece to the choker facing, right sides together. Stitch around the edges with a 1/2-in. seam. Trim seams and notch curves. Turn to the right side and press. Fold the raw edges of the straight side to the inside of the choker and pin them. Then stitch across the end.

Try the choker on over your shirt and mark where it overlaps for a comfortable fit. The rounded end should overlap the straight end. Pin the hook-and-loop tape patches in place to form a loop. Stitch around the edges of the patches twice.

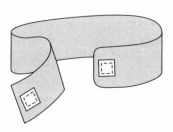

WESTERN SHIRT DESIGN IDEAS

Western shirts are worn by rodeo, reining, and cutting competitors and by men in Western show classes. They are, of course, very popular casual attire as well. You can use many different fabric patterns and colors in combination with the traditional yokes and pockets to create a variety of styles and effects.

Stripes and plaids are the traditional fabrics for Western shirts, but you can vary the direction of the stripe or plaid among the pattern pieces. Stripes on the front pockets can be matched exactly with the stripes on the shirt front, as shown in the drawing. Or you can cut the torso, pockets, yokes, and front band so that their stripes are diagonal, while the stripes on the sleeves of the shirt are vertical. The collar and sleeves might then have horizontal stripes. You can vary the combinations in many ways.

Also, you can add a solid-color yoke to a striped or plaid shirt, or vice versa.

Color-blocked shirts, using two colors of fabric, are dramatic and fun to make. Again, many combinations are possible.

Another two-color design variation is a shirt with the front in a light color and the rest of the shirt a dark color, as shown in the drawing.

CHAPTER 7

CHAPS

Chaps are leather or suede items worn over pants as leg protection, and are worn exclusively for horseback riding — with the exception of motorcycle chaps. They can be strictly functional items or can have a lot of creative flair. Chaps come in two basic styles — shotgun and batwing. Chinks, which are shorter versions of batwing chaps, and gaiters, are variations of chaps.

MATERIALS AND NOTIONS

Traditional chaps are made from suede or smooth leather. Work or schooling chaps that are worn all day and every day should be made from heavier chap suede or 4 oz. to 5 oz. leather. Chaps that are not worn as often, such as show chaps and schooling chaps for riders on a lighter schedule, are usually made of medium-weight chap suede of 2 1/2-3 oz. Real leather is durable and gives extra grip in the saddle. Because it is a skin, it breathes, but it also provides warmth. It can be washed, though only with care and not very frequently. Leather can also be dry-cleaned, although this tends to be expensive.

Show chaps can also be made from a heavy-weight synthetic suede, such as Ultrasuede. Synthetic suede is available in more colors than real leather and can be machine-washed and dried. It is very easy to sew and is more comfortable to wear in warmer weather. Ultrasuede has a high cost per yard, but compared to buying a pair of custom-made chaps, the total cost is reasonable. Ultrasuede is not as durable as real leather, however, and you have to back it with fusible interfacing.

You can find notions such as zippers, buckles, and conchos, at leather stores and mail-order companies. (Sources for leather and notions are listed in Appendix II.)

ZIPPERS

Leather chaps should be made with heavy-duty chap zippers with metal teeth. Unfortunately, these zippers usually only come in brown and black, and sometimes the length selection is limited. You can use a zipper that is 1 in. to 2 in. shorter than the pattern calls for if that's all you can find.

Sometimes, suppliers sell zipper tape cut to length. You then buy a separate zipper pull, top and bottom stops, and assemble the zipper yourself (the assembly is not difficult). This way, you can get the exact length you need.

For Ultrasuede chaps you can use zippers with plastic teeth. These are available in a much wider range of lengths and colors and are also sold in cut-to-length tapes. Suppliers of outerwear and activewear fabrics usually sell them.

Install chap zippers so that they zip from the top of the leg down.

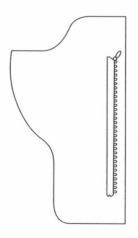

BUCKLES

Buckles for chaps should also be heavy-duty. Chaps buckles come in a range of sizes, depending on the belt width. They are usually made of solid brass, with a choice of a polished-brass, nickel, or sterling-silver finish, as well as combinations of these, with or without gold accents.

A very nice feature for fancy show chaps is to use a matching set of buckle, keeper (the loop that holds the end of the belt), and belt tip for the front belt. Many styles are available from tack and Western wear stores and leather suppliers. English schooling chaps and some work chaps will need a back buckle in addition to a smaller front buckle.

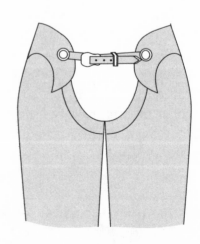

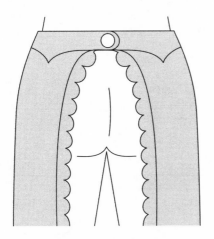

ONE CONCHO BACK

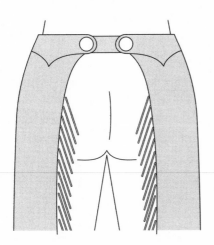

TWO CONCHO BACK

CONCHOS

Western show chaps are usually attached at the back with one or two conchos. Fashion, to some extent, dictates whether one or two used; body size is another consideration.

A two-concho back fits a large person better and a one-concho back fits a small person better. If you are using two conchos on chaps for a large person, make the yoke extensions longer and the back belt piece shorter so that the conchos will be closer together. This will help to visually decrease the body width.

Conchos are usually made of sterling silver over brass, and they have screw-post backs to attach them to the belt. Choose a size that is appropriate for the width of the belt.

Rather than using conchos, another option is to cover a large button or buttons with the same material as the chaps (see Appendix II for a company that will do this).

FITTING

When sewing chaps, fitting is everything. I highly recommend making a test pair from canvas, nonwoven interfacing, or felt to fine-tune the fit. Once the chap sides are cut out, there is very little you can do to alter them. Choose a material for the test pair that resembles your actual chap material in weight and drape.

Take the following body measurements, as shown in drawing, while wearing the pants that will be worn under the chaps:

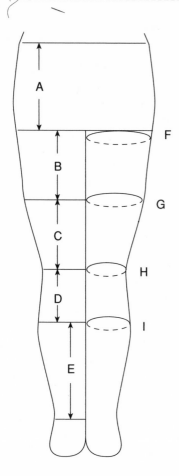

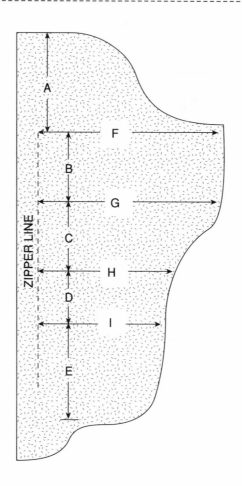

A. Chap top (where you want the chap to ride) to crotch
B. Crotch to thigh
C. Thigh to knee
D. Knee to calf

E. Calf to boot instep
F. Leg circumference at crotch
G. Leg circumference at midthigh
H. Leg circumference at knee
I. Leg circumference at calf

Compare these to the corresponding areas of the chap-side pattern piece and alter the pattern as needed. You'll need a little ease at the knee, but otherwise the chap measurements should match the body measurements.

Western show chaps should fit perfectly. The top of the chap should come to the waistline so that the chap belt covers your pants belt. The crotch edge of the chap should be at the top of the inner thigh. The chap sides should be wide enough at the hips so that the outer half of the buttocks is covered. The chaps should lie smoothly in front and not gape. To correct a front that doesn't lie smoothly, make the front edge wider. The top of the chap zipper should start high, above the level of the saddle when you're sitting on a horse. The zipper should then run smoothly down the outer side back of your leg, not the back of your leg. The chaps should also be long enough to cover the boot heel when you're sitting on the horse.

After altering the pattern, cut out the chap pieces from your test material and baste in the zippers. Try the test chaps on over your show pants, belt, and buckle. Make any needed changes to the pattern pieces before cutting the leather or Ultrasuede for the final pair.

Large people or women with small waists and larger hips and thighs present common fitting problems. On more curved body types, the chap zipper tends to twist instead of lying flat and straight down the leg. I've talked to quite a few custom-chap makers, and unfortunately there is no magic solution. Simply make a test pair and experiment with changing the curve of the inside chap edge to find the best fit.

CHAP STYLES

There are two chaps styles: shotgun and batwing. Shotgun chaps are more form-fitting and have a zipper on the outside of the leg. They are worn for English and Western schooling and in some Western show classes. Batwing chaps have wider legs and buckle around the thigh. They are worn in cutting horse classes, in rodeos. and by working cowboys. Both types of chaps can be belted with buckles at the back and/or the front of the waist.

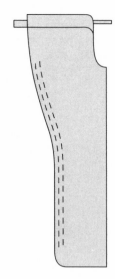

ENGLISH SCHOOLING CHAP

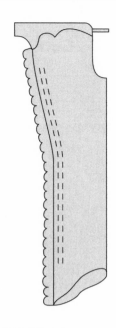

WESTERN SHOW CHAP

Shotgun-style English schooling chaps usually have simple yoke designs and have both back and front belts. They usually do not have fringe and have little or no drop. They are made from smooth or suede leather.

Western show chaps are also shotgun style, but generally have a longer "drop," that is, the portion that hangs below the boot when the rider is in the saddle. The yokes range from simple to very ornate. They often have matching cuffs, and are fastened in the front with a narrow strap and buckle. The back belt of Western show chaps is held together with one or two conchos or a large covered button. There are other yoke and belt variations.For example, the yokes and back can be one piece. A variation is the "reiner" chap, where the yokes and front are one piece. Western show chaps are usually fringed, though sometimes they are also scalloped. The fringe can be on the leg only or continue around the bottom of the back belt area. Western show chaps are usually made from suede leather or synthetic suede.

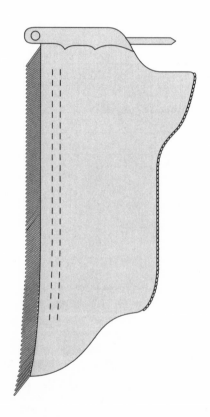

WESTERN SHOW CHAP

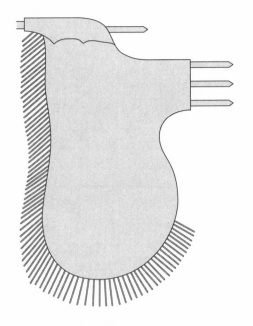

BATWING CHAP

Batwing chaps are similar to shotgun chaps, in that they have yoked front and back belts. The leg is wider, however, and is buckled around the wearer's leg. The side edge and sometimes the bottom edge of the batwing chap can be fringed. Chinks are short batwing chaps that end at the knee. The bottom and side edges are usually fringed.

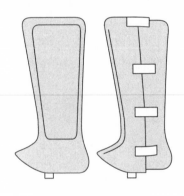

GAITERS

Gaiters, or half chaps, are shaped pieces of leather that fasten around the lower leg with Velcro strips. They have an extra layer of leather on the inside of the leg, and are worn with short boots or shoes to protect the leg from chafing.

SEWING LEATHER

Leather is usually sold in half-hide pieces, called sides, and the price is based on the area of the piece, measured in square feet. The best way to select hides is to take your pattern to the leather store. The store personnel will help you lay out your pattern on the actual hides so that you can choose your material efficiently.

Leather has lengthwise and crosswise grain. The lengthwise grain runs along the backbone of the hide. As much as possible, place the chap side and belt pieces on the thickest center part of the hide. You can place the yokes and cuffs farther to the outside. The top edge

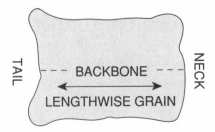

of the chap sides should be at the neck edge of the hide.

Leather is a natural product, so it will have surface blemishes and holes. Make sure that you can fit all the pattern pieces on areas that don't have major imperfections. You will probably have to live with some minor flaws unless you're willing to buy enough leather to place all the pattern pieces on perfect areas. If possible, place the back sections of the chaps on the less perfect parts of the hide.

If you cannot fit the entire chap on one hide, cut the chap pattern in two pieces at the area above the knee. Add seam allowances. Overlap the pieces, matching the seam lines, and glue them together with rubber cement. Sew two rows of stitching as shown in the drawing. (You can make the chap in two pieces even if you don't need to, to create a decorative look.)

If you have to buy leather through the mail, first lay out your pattern pieces and try to estimate the square footage. Your mail-order supplier should be able help you decide how many hides you need. It's a good idea to order extra if you're not sure so that all of your hides are from the same dye lot. The supplier will usually send you hides from the same dye lot, but it doesn't hurt to ask. If you end up with an extra hide, the supplier should let you return it, but check this, too, before you buy.

Once you have purchased the hides, prepare them for cutting. Press them with a warm, dry iron. It is very important that the iron be dry, because steam can discolor the leather. Use a press cloth or brown paper between your iron and the hide. Identify any imperfections on the right side of the hide and mark them on the wrong side with tailor's chalk.

Cut the pattern pieces from a single layer of hide, with the wrong side up. Lay out the pattern pieces, remembering that you will lay out one side (either the right or left), cut these

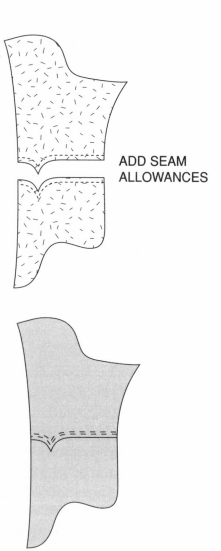

ADD SEAM
ALLOWANCES

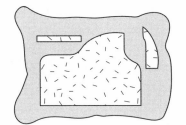
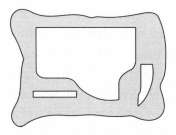

pieces, and then flip the pattern pieces over to cut the opposite side. After determining where all the pieces should go, tape the first set of pattern pieces in place. Next, cut them out, using a nice, sharp pair of shears or a rotary cutter. The cut edges should be perpendicular to the leather surface, not beveled. After one set of pattern pieces is cut out, flip the pieces over, tape them in place on the hide, and cut the other set of pieces out. Use tailor's chalk to transfer the pattern markings to the wrong side of the leather.

Leather is actually easy to sew on the typical home sewing machine. Before doing anything with your precious leather pieces, however, experiment with some scraps and different needles and threads to find what works best with your machine. Regular needles can sometimes tear the hide, but you can buy special leather needles with triangular points that cleanly cut the leather. I have never gotten the leather needles to work well with my machine, however, and a leather expert I know says she never uses them either. I've used needles intended for woven and knit fabrics and have never had problems. So it's best to experiment.

You'll need large needles, such as Size 16, for heavy leather and smaller needles, such as Size 14, for lighter leather, as well as polyester or cotton-covered polyester thread. Try stitching on both single and double layers of leather with a stitch length of 7 to 9 stitches per inch, using the longer length for heavier leather. Reduce the presser-foot tension, if necessary, when working with heavy leather. If the stitching is too loose or too tight or forms loops, adjust the upper tension. If you have problems feeding the leather evenly in your machine, try a special roller or Teflon foot. Stitch slowly and practice stitching exactly where you want to. Once you stitch the real thing, you create permanent holes in the leather, and so you do not want to rip out incorrect stitching.

To "baste" pieces together before stitching, apply rubber cement lightly so that the excess does not squeeze out. Again, stitch carefully, and avoid backstitching, if possible. When you've finished sewing, leave long thread ends, pull them to the wrong side, and knot them securely. Then cut off excess thread ends.

MAKING CHAP FRINGE

Fringe is the most popular optional feature for Western show chaps. Because swinging fringe will emphasize any leg movement when you are riding, most show chaps have narrow fringe, which tends to be "quieter." Unfortunately, this makes the onerous task of cutting fringe even more time-consuming.

The easiest and most accurate way to cut fringe is to use a rotary cutter and a rigid, see-through ruler. You can place the ruler so that you get the same fringe width for every piece of fringe. The rotary cutter makes a nice, straight cut and saves wear and tear on the hand muscles.

SCHOOLING CHAPS WITH CONTRAST EDGING

Edging in a contrasting color makes a very attractive pair of chaps.

After determining the fit and making alterations to the pattern pieces, draw a line 1/2 in.

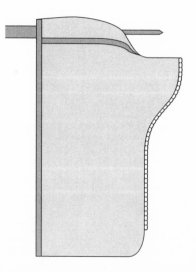

from the front side edge of the chap side piece, and remove this much of the chap pattern.

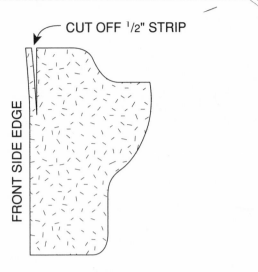

CUT OFF ¹/₂" STRIP

FRONT SIDE EDGE

Cut out all chap pieces from the main color of leather. Use the front yoke pattern as a template to draw a line parallel to and ¹/₂ in. above the lower edge of the front yoke piece. Then draw a matching line 1 in. from the first (¹/₂ in. below the lower edge of the yoke). The 1-in.-wide area between these two lines is the new pattern piece for the yoke edging. Cut a paper pattern of this section.

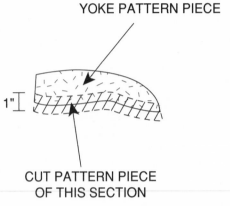

YOKE PATTERN PIECE

1"

CUT PATTERN PIECE
OF THIS SECTION

Measure the length of the front edge of the chap side piece. Then, on the lengthwise grain, cut two 1-in.-wide strips this length from the contrasting color of leather.

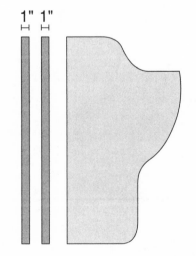

1" 1"

Cut two front yoke-edging pieces from the contrasting leather, remembering to cut two opposite shapes. Place the front yokes on top of the yoke edging, overlapping by ¹/₂ in. This leave ¹/₂ in. of the edging exposed. Glue the pieces in place.

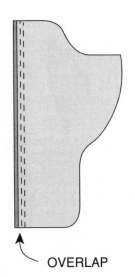

OVERLAP

Place the 1-in.-wide strips underneath the chap front side edges, overlapping them by 1/2 in., and glue them in place. Stitch them down close to the chap edge, and then stitch again 1/4 in. from the first line of stitching.

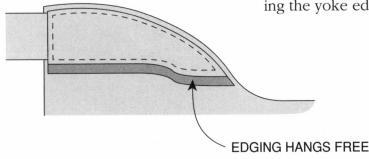

EDGING HANGS FREE

Construct the chaps following the pattern instructions. Then sew the front yokes on, leaving the yoke edging free.

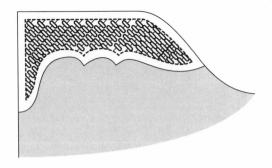

WESTERN SHOW CHAP DESIGN IDEAS

It's currently popular to have a tooled, smooth leather yoke on suede chaps. You can hand-tool the yoke yourself (see Appendix II for sources of leatherworking supplies). Keep in mind that this type of yoke draws attention to the hip area.

It's easy to add custom-designed yokes and cuffs to a basic chap pattern. Lay out the chap pattern with the yoke pinned in place. Draw the new yoke and cuff shapes on the pattern. Lay a piece of tracing paper on top and transfer the new designs. Make the chaps following the pattern instructions, using the new pieces.

Reiner chaps are another newly popular style. They have a wide, solid front and are

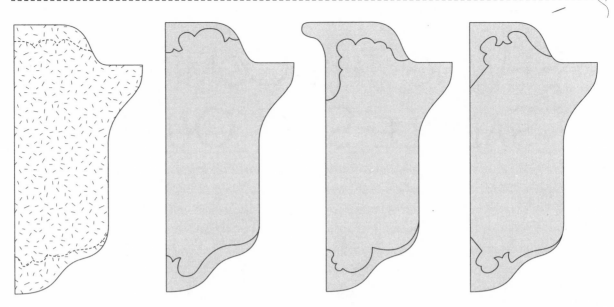

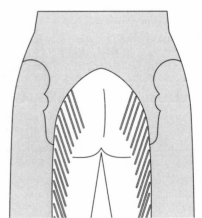

particularly flattering for large riders. Another option is a one-piece back. Instead of the back's being connected with conchos, the front yokes and back are all one piece. This is an attractive look for riders with long torsos. Both of these styles require extra care in fitting.

CARE AND CLEANING

You can take leather chaps to dry cleaners that specialize in cleaning leather, but it's expensive, so you might do it only once a year. Some people machine-wash their leather chaps on a gentle cycle in lukewarm water with nondetergent soap. If possible, remove buckles and conchos before washing. Then air-dry the chaps on a flat surface. The leather will be stiff when it dries, but can be softened by rubbing it with your hand.

Ultrasuede chaps can be machine-washed in the same way, then machine-dried on low heat. Another option is to air-dry the chaps until they are almost dry, and then put them briefly in the dryer.

CHAPTER 8

SEWING THE COMPLETE SADDLE-SEAT OUTFIT

All of the elements of the saddle-seat outfit — coat, vest, shirt, and jodhpurs — must be coordinated for proper fit.

Coats for saddle-seat riding come in two basic styles. The saddle-suit coat has notched lapels and is worn with a matching vest and jodhpurs. The daycoat has a shawl collar and is worn with or without a vest. The daycoat style is also used for tuxedo-type coats for formal evening classes. Both coats have front pockets, center back vents, and are fastened with one button slightly above the waist. They are worn quite long. The back has either inverted or tucked deep pleats on either side of the center vent.

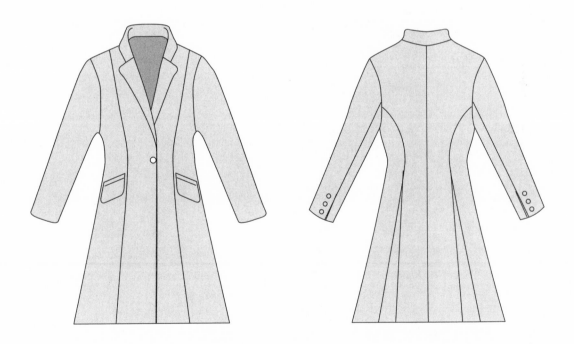

SADDLE SUIT COAT

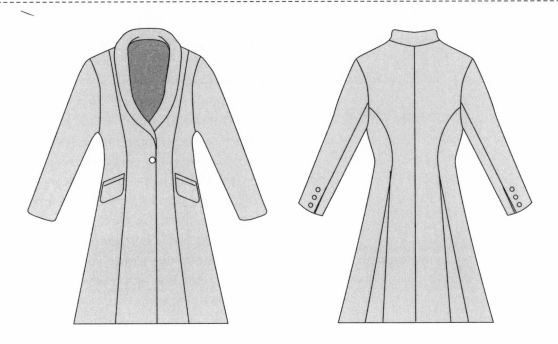

DAYCOAT

Fabric choices vary. Saddle-seat suits can be made from wool, wool blend, or synthetic suiting fabrics. Choose the most expensive fabric you can afford. The conservative colors for saddle-seat suits are dark solids, such as navy and brown, or muted pinstripes. Daycoats can be made from similar fabrics in bright colors and can also be made from silk suitings. Saddle suits are generally either all one color, or the vest and jodhpurs are the same color and the coat a lighter color. Daycoats are usually light colors with dark pants. If a vest is worn with a daycoat, it can match the pants or even be a plaid.

Color combinations depend upon the breed of horse, the type of horse-show class, and current fashion. Attend shows to see what others are wearing and consult with trainers and friends who show. Also be sure to know what the rulebook specifies for your breed and also consider the show venue. If you show primarily in indoor arenas, choose lighter colors so that you show up better, and darker colors when showing outside.

If you need both a suit and a daycoat, consider using the same jodhpurs with both coats. Make the suit in a solid dark color and choose daycoat fabric that will coordinate with the pants of the suit. I know a woman who made a navy suit for her daughter and then made a daycoat from a lilac raw-silk fabric shot through with threads of purples and blues.

Saddle-seat coats should fit well. The most important consideration is how the coat looks on the rider when riding. The back should fit smoothly and not pull. The sleeves should be long enough so that they touch the wristbone when the arms are in the riding position.

For women and children, the coat should hang below the knee when standing, though length variations exist depending upon breed and also upon the rider's build. For men, the coat is usually worn a bit shorter — slightly above the knee. The back vent should begin at or slightly below the waist. Lapel widths change according to current trends, but a medium-width lapel is always correct. If a vest is being worn with the coat, try on both the vest and the coat to evaluate the fit.

One consideration when making the saddle-suit coat is that, when the rider is riding, the bottom front of the coat opens up so that the lining shows (as shown in the drawing on p. 76). This means that the front facing should not be too wide, to allow the lining to show, and also that you must choose the color of the lining with care. You can choose a contrasting color for an extra accent or a coordinating color. If using a lining color that is lighter than the coat color, make sure that the coat seams and interfacing do not show through the lining fabric. (See Chapter 4 for hints on sewing a tailored coat.)

The vest worn with the saddle suit is the same style as the standard men's suit vest. It should be fitted to have a smooth appearance under the coat.

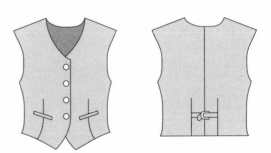

SADDLE SUIT VEST

A standard dress shirt is worn with the saddle-seat outfit; tuxedo shirts are also worn with formal suits. Cotton and cotton-blend shirting with woven sew-in interfacings are good fabric choices. A white shirt is always correct, though in some informal classes you will see pastel colors. Because the shirt collar is almost the only part of the shirt that shows, it is important that it fit well. A small section of the shirt cuff (1/8 in. to 1/4 in.) should extend beyond the coat sleeve when the rider's arms are in the riding position. If the shirt does not fit smoothly through the torso, you can add darts to take in excess fabric. (See Chapter 6 for more information about sewing and fitting riding shirts.)

Saddle-seat jodhpurs, also called Kentucky jods, are quite different from the breeches and jodhpurs worn by the sport-horse disciplines. They are similar in construction to men's suit trousers. They should be fitted at the waist, loose through the hips and crotch (which don't show when wearing the coat), and fitted through the leg with enough ease in the knee for riding comfort. The bottoms of the jodhpurs are flared at the boot, as shown in the drawing. The hemline slopes from front to back, ending up with a point at the back so the hem hangs correctly. The pant hem should touch the boot in front and cover the heel in back. Elastic straps are buttoned to the inside of the pants hem to prevent the pant legs from riding up. (You can also buy jodhpur straps.)

Because jodhpurs that are the correct length for riding will drag on the ground when you're walking, you need a way to hold up the hem when you're not on your horse. If your jodhpurs have tabs for buttoning on foot straps, you can sew buttons on the inside of the hem. You then would turn up the hems to the inside and button them to the tabs. Another option is simply to sew hooks and eyes to the inside of the pants to hold the hem up at the correct length.

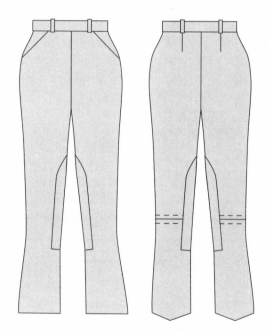

SADDLE SUIT JODHPURS

Because your jodhpurs experience more wear, they will probably wear out before your coat does. Buy enough fabric to make two pairs, and you'll extend the life of your show outfit.

You can sew two other types of jodhpurs. The first type is worn for in-hand classes. Working with the same jodhpur pattern, take in the side seams at the hip area for a more fitted look. Also, shorten the pants to cover the boot in back and to rest on the boot instep in front. (You might have to shorten the pattern between the knee and the hem to keep the correct shape of the pants leg.) To save time and money, you can simply wear your riding jodhpurs and turn up the hem, as described above, to secure the hems at the correct length. For in-hand classes, wear jodhpurs with a shirt and vest.

You can also sew jodhpurs for schooling at home, of the same style as show jodhpurs. A nice option is to use a slightly stretchy fabric, such as stretch gabardine, which makes a comfortable pair of jodhpurs.

HEMMING JODHPURS

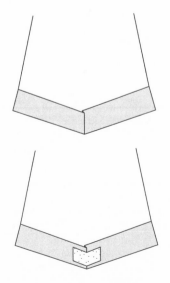

Before sewing, you should adjust the hems of the jodhpurs, as decribed above. The rider should be sitting on the horse and wearing show boots. (If you're the rider, have a helper adjust the hem.) The hem should curve very slightly from front to back. Then fold the hem in a tuck at the back to form the correct point, as shown in the drawing.

You can hand-stitch a piece of stiff interfacing to the hem at the heel, as shown in the drawing. This will help the hem to hang correctly and maintain the proper shape.

KNEE REINFORCEMENTS

Saddlesuit jodhpurs have knee reinforcements made from the pants material, or for better durability, from Ultrasuede or even suede leather. Keep in mind that some dry cleaners will not accept garments with real leather. (See Chapter 5 for more information about sewing leather patches.)

SEWING THE FORMAL SADDLE SUIT

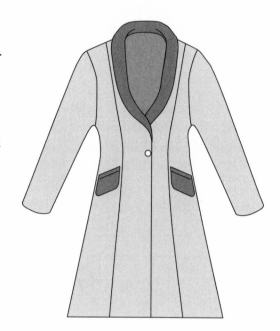

A tuxedo version of the saddle suit is worn for many formal evening classes. To make a tuxedo suit, choose a saddle-suit coat pattern with a shawl collar. Use a black suiting material for the coat and jodhpurs and a heavy black satin for the front facing, upper collar, and pocket flaps and welts. You'll also sew a satin stripe down the side of the jodhpurs. Equitation riders can also choose dark gray, dark brown, or midnight blue for formal suits, though black is the traditional choice.

Measure the length of the jodhpur side seams. Cut two 2-in.-wide strips of black satin to this length, making sure to cut the strips on the lengthwise grain. For very small or large sizes, you might want to make the satin strips narrower or wider to make them more proportionate to the width of the pants leg.

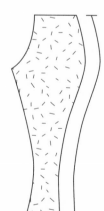

MEASURE LENGTH
OF SIDE SEAM

1"

Press under 1/2 in. on each long side of the strips.

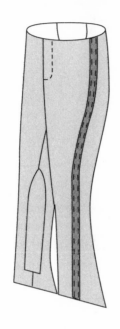

After sewing and pressing the jodhpur side seams, and before putting on the waistband, pin the strips over the side seams. Topstitch close to each long edge, beginning at the top of the pants. Because you've probably already sewn the inseam, this step can get tricky as you stitch farther down the leg. Make sure you keep the section you are stitching flat, so that you don't catch any other part of the pants.

The formal saddle suit is worn with a tuxedo shirt, bow tie, and cummerbund or waistcoat.

CHAPTER 9

SEWING THE COMPLETE WESTERN SHOW OUTFIT

Whether you go to a major horse show of the stock breeds or Western classes of other breed shows, the variety of show apparel can be overwhelming. The fashion trend-setting venue for Quarter Horse, Appaloosa, and Paint competitors is the U.S. Quarter Horse Congress in Columbus, Ohio, which is held every October. These days you see everything from classic tailored elegance to wild patterns, color, and glitter. Morgan, Arabian, and open Western classes have their own trends, which can be equally as confusing.

When planning an outfit to sew, how can you choose from all the options available? The first step is to know what is required by the official rules of the organizations governing your shows. If you are showing at local non-sanctioned shows, you might not have to worry about the technicalities, but you can't go wrong if you follow the rules anyway. The next step is to find out the latest trends for your breed of horse. Fashions also vary regionally, especially from East Coast to West Coast. If possible, go to lots of shows, talk to trainers and friends who show, and read publications. *Horse and Rider* magazine has frequent articles about show-ring style for both the rider and the horse.

Once you have a good knowledge of the options, the next step is to decide what will work best for you and your horse. When at shows, try to find riders who have builds similar to yours and ride horses of similar color to yours. See what looks good on these combinations. Keep in mind that your horse presents a large block of color in the show ring, and your outfit should coordinate with this color.

Consult your library for books on fashion colors. Bright colors will attract attention. If you ride one of the breeds with a flashy coat, choose an outfit that doesn'tclash. Conventional wisdom says not to wear red tones on an orange-toned horse (such as a chestnut) and not to wear orange tones on a red-toned horse. These rules can be broken, however, if you find the right shades. Also consider whether you'll be showing inside or out. Subdued colors in a large indoor arena can make you almost disappear.

When in doubt, choose an outfit that is simple, conservative, and workmanlike. Your clothes and your horse's tack should be neat, clean, and well fitting. You want to present a professional, competent image. The most important thing is that you feel good about the way you look. Even if your trainer, your best friend, and your spouse tell you that a certain trendy color is the only way to go, don't do it if the color makes you cringe. Your outfit should do everything to make you feel like a winner when you enter the show ring, and nothing about it should detract from your performance.

A very fitted, smooth look is the current trend in Western show classes. All the components should fit smoothly, with no gapes, puckers, or flapping parts. To achieve a smooth look, add darts to shirts and blouses to take in excess fabric. Choose patterns with princess seams in the front and back for a very fitted look. Use zippers either instead of or underneath buttoned openings. Current jacket styles are waist-length or slightly below the waist, which allows the fit to be very trim. Another style option that creates a smooth appearance is a shirt or blouse made as a bodysuit.

WESTERN SHOW BLOUSES, VESTS, AND JACKETS

Some of the options for women competitors are shirts or blouses, vests worn over a shirt, a short jacket worn over a shirt, and shirt jackets that combine elements of both.

One popular style is the fitted blouse with stand-up collar. The blouse has bust and waist darts and is very close fitting. It also has a zipper in the back and shoulder pads. The sleeves can be slightly gathered at the shoulder and the cuff. The blouse can also be made as a bodysuit. You can use almost any woven fabric. Many variations of yoke styles, appliques, pleats, and fabric combinations are possible.

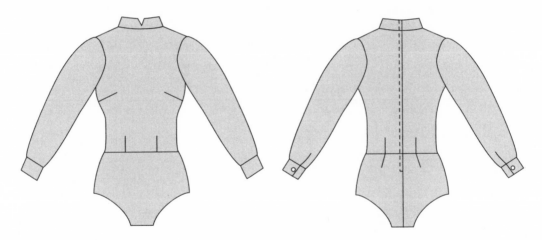

WESTERN SHOW BODYSUIT

To prevent buttoned shirts and blousesfrom gaping, sew a zipper under the center front and add buttons on top. You can also fasten shirt and blouse cuffs with hook-and-loop tape, and sew the cuff button or buttons on the outside of the cuff. This is a good idea for those of you who have to make quick tack and apparel changes between horse-show classes.

Vest designs are fairly standard. They have darts or princess seams and are very close fitting. To vary the look, you can add a little collar to the front of the vest. Some makers of

WESTERN SHOW VEST

custom show apparel advocate making the
back of the vest in the vest fabric instead of
the usual lining fabric. A back of lining fabric
breaks up the look of the vest as the horse and
rider pass from front to back view. The vest
should be long enough in back to cover your
belt when you are in the saddle; the front
points should fit over your belt so that the
buckle shows.

The fitted short jacket is another very popular option. You can choose from many neckline styles, such as notched and shawl collars,
jewel-necked, and collarless scoop necks. The
front can be single- or double-breasted, have
different button configurations, or be asymmet-
rical. These jackets are constructed using tailoring methods, so consult Chapter 4. As with
vests, the jacket back should cover your belt

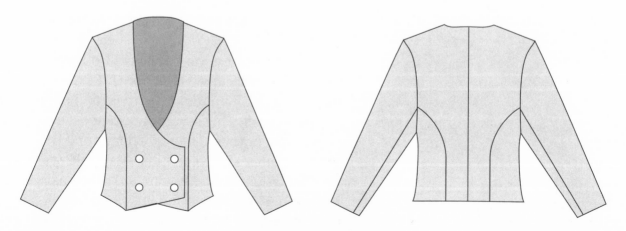

WESTERN SHOW JACKET

when you are in the saddle, and if there are front points they should fit over your belt so that the buckle shows.

You can use many different fabrics for vests and jackets, including heavy raw silk, brocades, tapestry fabric, metallics, and Ultrasuede, in addition to more conventional fabrics such as wool and wool blends. Beaded and sequinned fabrics are currently popular, especially on the national show circuits.

CONVERTING A BLOUSE TO A BODYSUIT

A show blouse can be converted to a body-suit fairly easily. Buy a pair of underpants that have a top edge that is at least 2 in. below your waistline — some bikini styles work well.

While wearing both garments, pin the blouse to the panties below the top elastic edge. Provide enough blouse fabric above the panties to allow lengthwise ease for sitting and bending, but maintaining as smooth a fit as possible. Mark the overlap of fabric on the blouse and panties and then add seam allowances before cutting.

Cut off the top elastic of the panties. Also cut off the excess lower section of the blouse, allowing enough for seam allowances on both the panties and blouse. Finish the raw bottom edge of the blouse to prevent the fabric from raveling.

PIN BLOUSE BELOW ELASTIC

LEAVE ENOUGH FOR SEAM ALLOWANCES

If the blouse has a buttoned front, match the center fronts at the bottom and stitch an X-in-a-box above the seamline, as shown in the drawing. To make an X-in-a-box, stitch a 1-in. square, then stitch diagonal lines from the corners of the square.

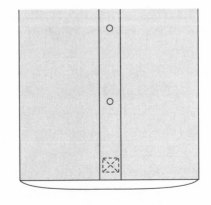

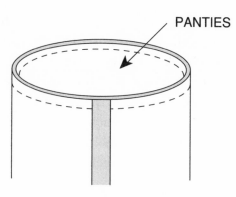

PANTIES

Turn the blouse inside out and insert the panties. With right sides together, pin the bottom blouse edge to the top panties edge, stretching the panties just enough to allow the lower edge of the blouse to fit smoothly, and stitch.

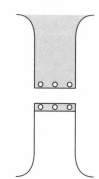

To add sew-on snaps or snap tape, slit the front of the crotch section (be sure the snaps will be in a comfortable position!).

SEWING BEADED AND SEQUINNED FABRICS

Showy glitter fabrics with beads and sequins definitely put you in the spotlight in the show ring, but require some special sewing techniques. Choose a garment pattern that is as simple as possible, with a minimum of seams.

Obviously, you can't use fusible interfacing as you would for most vests and jackets. For structured-looking garments, use sew-in interfacing. Cut all of the bodice pieces and sleeve pieces (for a jacket) from the interfacing and machine-baste them to the wrong side of the fabric pieces. Do not use facing pieces for the front and back neck; instead, line the entire inside of the garment. Choose a lining fabric that matches the garment fabric in weight.

If you want a softer look, don't use interfacing at all — just line the entire garment. This method is appropriate for very simple, slightly less fitted shirt jackets. Use only lightweight sequinned or beaded fabrics, however. Heavy fabrics will sag without interfacing.

Sequinned and beaded fabrics do have a nap and should be cut from a single layer. Prepare the fabric by pressing it on the wrong side with a warm, dry iron. Place pins in the seam allowances or use pattern weights. Remember to reverse the pattern pieces to cut the right and left sides of the garment. (Cutting these fabrics will really dull your shears, so use an older pair if possible.) Sequins are usually attached to the base fabric with a chain stitch that will easily unravel if you accidentally pull a loose thread. To keep the fabric from unraveling, wrap tape around the cut edges after you cut out the pattern pieces from the fabric.

Use a small needle and change needles frequently, because stitching these fabrics rapidly dulls the needle. If you're making a lined vest or jacket, plain seams are appropriate. If your sequinned or beaded fabric is quite heavy, however, consider removing the sequins or beads from the seam allowances to reduce bulk. The garment will be more comfortable to wear without bulky and scratchy seam allowances poking you through the lining. To do this, first mark the seam lines on the wrong side of the pattern pieces. Then carefully remove the sequins or beads from the seam allowances plus 1/8 in. Knot the threads to prevent them from unraveling. Apply tape to hold the sequins or beads out of the way of the seam lines and stitch the seam with right sides together. As when cutting out, try to place pins only in the seam allowances.

SEWING A REVERSIBLE VEST OR JACKET

One way to extend your show wardrobe without spending much extra money or time is to make a reversible vest or jacket. For a jacket to be reversible, it must be collarless and the

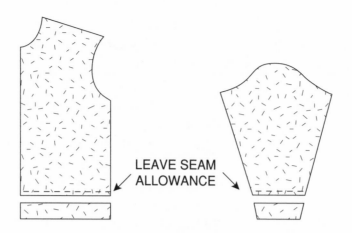

LEAVE SEAM
ALLOWANCE

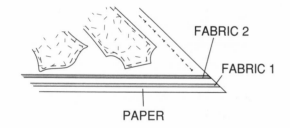

FABRIC 2

FABRIC 1

PAPER

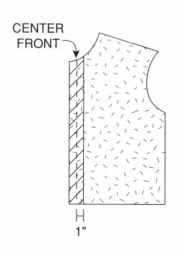

CENTER
FRONT

H
1"

fabrics for the two sides should be of the same weight. Using the same fabric in different colors is an excellent solution, or you can use a solid color for one side and a print for the other. Medium-weight fabrics work best.

In place of facing and lining pieces, you will cut a duplicate set of vest or jacket pieces from each fabric. First cut off the hems from the pattern pieces, leaving a normal seam-allowance width.

Lay out the folded fabrics on tracing paper, one piece of fabric on the other, matching the folded edges. Pin the folded edges to the edge of the paper. You will have four layers of fabric pinned to one layer of paper. This technique keeps all the layers aligned on the straight grain.

Pin the pattern pieces in place, once again pinning through all layers including the paper. Pattern weights will help. Cut out the pieces. The reason for cutting all layers together is to have the two sides of the garment match as perfectly as possible.

You will not interface the entire front of the garment because this would make it too heavy and stiff. Instead, cut two strips of interfacing to cover 1 in. of the garment at the center front edges — cut strips for both sides. If using fusible interfacing, which I recommend, it is very important that you first test-fuse the interfacing to the fabric to make sure that it doesn't form a visible ridge on the right side of the

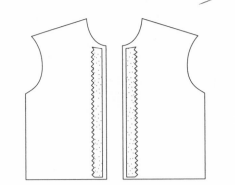

fabric. Also pink the inside edge of the interfacing strip. Pink one strip about 1/4 in. narrower than the other, so that the interfacing edges are staggered when the garment is constructed. This will help prevent a pressing line on the right side of the fabric. Fuse the strips to both the right and left front pieces on both sides of the garment.

If you're making a vest, you can now finish it using the normal construction techniques. When you turn the almost finished vest to the right side, make sure that the vest edges are aligned perfectly so that only one fabric is visible from each side. Roll the edges between your finger and thumb to check this. Press well.

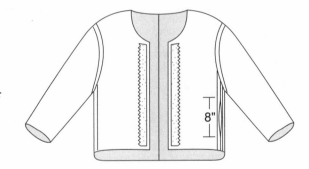

If you're making a jacket, construct the entire jacket from each of the two fabrics. Leave an 8-in. opening in the side seam of one of the jackets.

With **right sides** together, sew the front and neck edges of the two jackets together. Grade the seam allowances by trimming the allowances of one jacket to 1/4 in. and the seam allowances of the other slightly wider. Press all the seam allowances **open**.

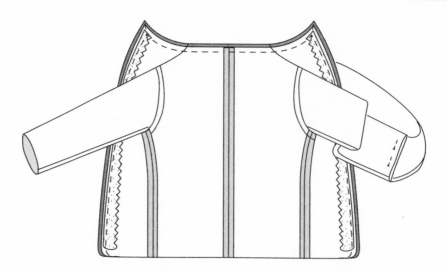

Turn the sleeves inside out. Fold back the ends of one set of sleeves about 2 in. Insert the folded-back sleeves into the ends of the other sleeves. Being very careful to match the correct sleeve seam or seams, pin the sleeve ends with **right sides together**. Stitch. Using a seam roll, press the seam allowances **open**.

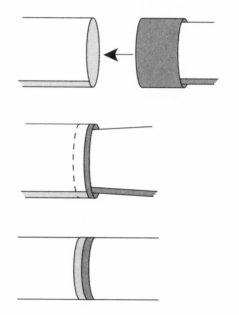

With **right sides together**, pin the hems of the jackets. Wrap all the center-edge seam allowances to one side or the other and stitch. Grade the seam allowances and press the seam open as much as possible.

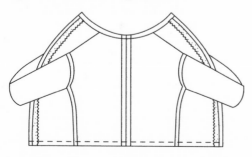

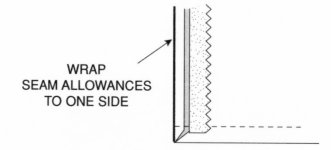

WRAP
SEAM ALLOWANCES
TO ONE SIDE

Pull the jacket to the right side through the 8-in. opening you left in one of the side seams. Now working inside the jacket, tack the armhole seam allowances together at the sleeve caps. This will keep the layers in place when you take off the jacket.

Make sure all of the corners and edges are completely pushed out and turned (use a pointer if you have one). Roll the jacket edges between your finger and thumb so that they are perfectly aligned. Press well.

Fold under the seam allowances and invisibly stitch together the side-seam opening.

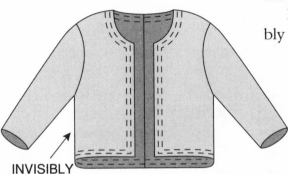

INVISIBLY
STITCH
OPENING

You can edgestitch a vest or jacket 1/8 in. from the edge to keep the edges nicely aligned. Use two colors of thread that match each side and a shorter stitch length. Make sure that the thread tension is equal for both upper and bobbin threads so that the stitching is uniform on both sides of the garment.

For a decorative touch, you can add more topstitching.

You'll probably want to have shoulder pads in the jacket. Cover the pads with a matching lining fabric and attach them with small safety pins that just catch the edges of the pads and the inside layer of the jacket fabric.

CHAPTER 10

SEWING OUTERWEAR

In recent years, long coats such as Western dusters and Australian outback coats have become popular. These coats are very functional for riding and can make dramatic fashion statements at the same time. Shorter jackets and slickers in a variety of styles and weights are also worn for riding. Features that are unique to riding coats include back vents that start at the waist, triangular saddle gussets sewn into the back vent to cover the saddle, and leg straps or snaps that keep the coats covering the leg.

FABRICS

The traditional Western duster is made of heavy cotton canvas in a natural unbleached off-white color. Both dusters and outback coats can be made in other colors of cotton canvas, cotton duck, denim, and other heavy-weight cotton-twill fabrics.

For added protection from the elements, you can use water- and wind-resistant fabrics. Totally waterproof fabrics, usually nylon coated with polyurethane or vinyl, do not breathe. Consequently, if you perspire while wearing them, you'll be hot and wet. Garments made from these fabrics are more comfortable if made loose fitting or are vented in some way. There are also partially water- and wind-resistant fabrics that are made from tightly woven nylon and nylon blends and sometimes are chemically treated. They are "breathable," and much more comfortable, but do not afford the same protection as totally waterproof fabric.

Goretex and Ultrex are among the newest type of outerwear fabric, sometimes advertised as breathable waterproof fabric. Depending on the manufacturer, these fabrics are either laminated or coated, and in theory, they only let water molecules travel in one direction — letting perspiration escape but keeping rainwater out. In practice, however, they are not 100 percent waterproof, nor are they breathable enough to let all the inner moisture escape. They are, however, an excellent and comfortable compromise, although they are more expensive than the other types of outerwear fabric.

The traditional fabric for Australian outback style coats is called oilcloth, oilskin, or waxed cloth. This fabric dates back to the late nineteenth century when fisherman soaked heavy cotton duck fabric in linseed oil so that the fabric would protect them from water and wind. The drawback was that the fabric eventually became very stiff. Over the years, manufacturers have developed improved processes for making oilcloth that do not have the disadvantages of the old method. Oilcloth is not readily available, but a source is listed in Appendix II.

Sewing with oilcloth has drawbacks. The oily finish can rub off, discoloring your hands and your cutting table. It can also clog your sewing machine. You have to change needles frequently. One woman told me that she had to have her entire sewing machine taken apart and cleaned each time she made an oilcloth coat, but she loved the final products so much she didn't mind. I know others who've used oilcloth, but whose machines did not get nearly as dirty. The last thing to consider is that oilcloth has a distinctive smell.

To add warmth or hide unfinished seams, you can add a lining to the coat. For warmth use wool or flannel, or a polyester bunting, such as Polarplus or Polarfleece, which is very warm but lightweight. For a traditional British look use a plaid design. If you do not need extra warmth, but would like a finished look on the inside, nylon lining fabric, such as taffe ta, is a good choice. Nylon is lightweight and slick, which makes the coat easy to slide on and off. Cotton fabrics should only be used for lining coats that will not get wet.

If you ride in very cold weather, you might consider insulating your coat. The most popular and readily available insulation is Thinsulate. As you can guess from its trade name, it is a very thin insulation. It is available in several different weights, from 1.3 to 6.5 oz./sq. yd. The medium weights are good choices for riding outerwear. Insulation similar to Thinsulate is available from other manufacturers.

Another type of insulation, called "high loft" and known by the trade names Hollofil and Quallofil, is designed to resemble goose down. Goose down is said to be warmer, but the synthetics have the advantages of — unlike down — being easy to handle and staying warm even when wet. These high-loft insulations produce puffy-looking coats. (Appendix II lists a company that sells sewing kits for making down coats as well as companies that sell patterns to use with synthetic insulations.)

NOTIONS

Outback coats and dusters require many snaps — usually $1/2$ in. in diameter. Because the correct installation of snaps is crucial to the appearance and function of the coat, it is a good idea to purchase a special snap-setting tool to do the job. Most snaps sold in fabric stores come with little tools, but these can be difficult to use. The tool is a short metal pin with a specially shaped end. A cupped "anvil" holds the snap, and the shaped end of the pin is placed onto the snap, which has a short hollow protruding cylinder. The pin is then tapped

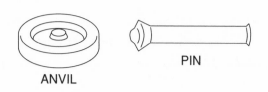

ANVIL   PIN

sharply with a hammer, which spreads the sides of the cylinder and fixes the snap in place. The short pin must be held perfectly vertically to set the snap correctly, which is awkward to do.

I can attest to having had many bruised thumbs before I bought a better snap-setting tool kit, called "The Snap-Setter." An extra tool securely holds the snap so that it is very easy to keep the pin in the correct position without risking injury. There are other snap-setting tool kits that simply have longer and sturdier pins and these are also easier to use.

A snap-setting kit also includes a hole punch, although you can buy better quality punches.

To install snaps, first pin together the parts of the coat where the snaps will be installed. For example, if you're installing front snaps in a duster, overlap the duster center fronts and pin them. Carefully mark the snap positions, and place the marked areas on a flat hard surface, protected by a scrap piece of wood. With the hole punch, punch holes in the exact center of the marked snap position through both layers of fabric. On fabrics that ravel, apply a sealing product, such as No-Fray.

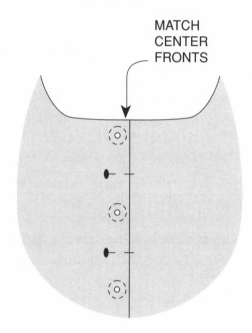

MATCH CENTER FRONTS

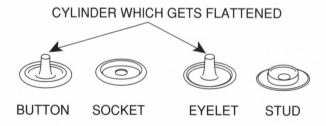

CYLINDER WHICH GETS FLATTENED

BUTTON   SOCKET   EYELET   STUD

Each snap consists of four parts. The top snap has a button section, which is the part of the snap that is visible on the outside of the garment. This attaches to a socket that is on the inside of the garment. The bottom snap has a stud section that is on the right side of the

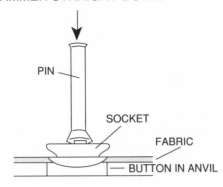

KEEP PIN VERTICAL-
HAMMER STRAIGHT DOWN

PIN

SOCKET

FABRIC

BUTTON IN ANVIL

coat and is attached to an eyelet that is on the inside of the coat. Each set has a small cylinder that sticks up and is flattened and spread to affix the snap. It is vital to insert the correct pieces in the correct positions.

Insert the button through the punched hole so that it is visible on the outside of the garment. Place the hole of the socket piece over the button cylinder sticking through the garment. If the fabric layers are thick, squeeze the snap pieces together as much as possible. Carefully holding the two pieces together, place the rounded surface of the button onto the anvil. Place the pin tool on top of the cylinder and tap it sharply with a hammer. If you do this correctly the sides of the cylinder will spread evenly. If the sides don't spread evenly or aren't flattened enough, tap again. Don't hammer too hard, however, or the button surface will distort. Because setting snaps correctly is definitely an acquired skill, I recommend you buy extra snaps and practice first on some fabric scraps.

Install the snap stud and eyelet the same way.

FITTING

Fitting coats is relatively easy. They are supposed to be quite loose-fitting because they are worn over other clothes. Choose a size that gives ample room through the chest and back. Before cutting out the fabric, check the back-neck-to-waist length, sleeve length, and hem length. Sleeves are often worn extra long on these coats.

STYLES OF COATS

The currently popular caped long coat is based on the Australian outback coat. The traditional Australian coat is long and fully cut with raglan sleeves, a rain cape, elbow patches, a front storm flap, snapped patch pockets, leg straps, a back saddle gusset, and a snapped collar tab. Everything that needs to be fastened — pockets, leg straps, collar strap, the coat front, rain cape, and back vent — is fastened with snaps.

Another traditional style of coat is the Western duster. This is a very long, straight-cut coat with set-in sleeves, Western yokes, and patch pockets. Corduroy often accents the collar and pocket flaps, and trims the yokes. The coat waist can be given shape with an inner drawstring or side tabs and D-rings. D-rings are metal D-shaped rings, usually 1 in. to 2 in. wide. One end of the belt is looped through the flat part of two rings and sewn; the other end is threaded through the middle of both rings and then between the round parts of the rings to lock the belt in place. Snaps are used as fasteners and can be installed on the front and back vent edges so that the coat can be snapped around the legs while riding. The traditional coat is long enough to drag on the ground when the wearer is standing, but you can install snaps to hold up the coat hem so that it doesn't.

There are many hybrid versions of these two coat styles, including three-quarter-length versions. You can pick and choose from any of the coat features to create the exact version you'd like.

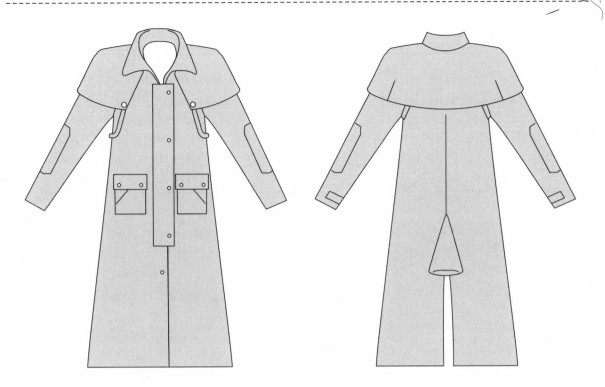

OUTBACK COAT

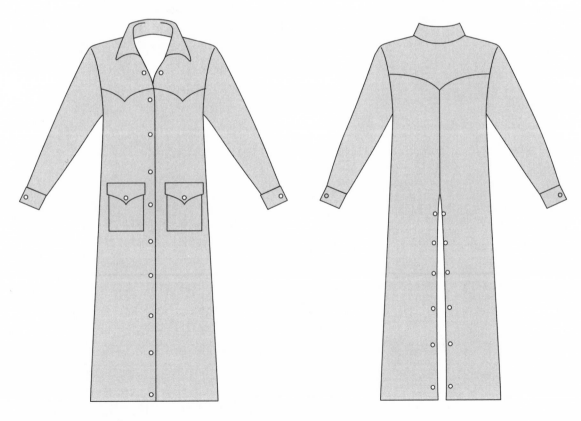

WESTERN DUSTER COAT

WATERPROOFING

When you stitch through a waterproof fabric, the needle holes can allow leaks in the finished garment. So, for full waterproofing of both breathable and nonbreathable waterproof fabrics, you need to seal the seams. Seam sealer, which is chemically similar to airplane glue, is usually available in tubes. If your fabric store doesn't carry it, you can find it at camping and backpacking outfitters. Follow the directions that come with the sealer, but generally you just apply a thin layer over all the stitching on the inside of the garment. For extra protection, I apply two layers. Be very careful and work only in a well-ventilated space because the fumes are very strong. If, after heavy wear, your coat begins to leak, apply more seam sealer. (Oilcloth doesn't need seam sealer; the impregnated cloth expands around the thread as it's stitched and seals the needle hole.)

If you're using a fabric that is not waterproof, a silicon spray, such as Scotchgard, will improve the water-resistance of the coat. You can even use it on canvas dusters. The spray has to be reapplied after the coat is cleaned, however.

MAKING AN INSULATED COAT

You can insulate both jackets and long coats, but the style needs to be simple and roomy enough to accommodate the insulation. The garment must also be fully lined, and both the outer coat fabric and lining should be tightly woven so that the insulation does not leak. Water-resistant nylon fabric is always a good choice for insulated coats. I made a lined outback coat with Ultrex and Thinsulate, and it's the warmest coat I've ever ridden in.

Purchase enough insulation material for all major pattern pieces, including the front, back, sleeves, and collar. If the coat has some type of front flap over the zipper, you can insulate this as well, although it must be faced to enclose the insulation.

The insulation can be applied to either the coat fabric or the lining fabric. It is usually applied to the lining so that the required rows of quilting stitches are not visible on the outside of the coat. For coat parts with both sides made from fabric, apply the insulation to one of the fabric sections rather than to a lining piece.

Cut out all the pattern pieces in both the coat fabric and the lining.

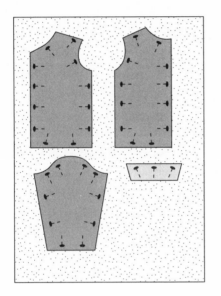

Lay out the insulation in a single layer. Some insulations, such as Thinsulate, have a smooth side and a fuzzy side. If this is the case, lay out the insulation with the fuzzy side facing up. Assuming you are applying insulation to the lining, place all appropriate lining pieces **right side up** on the insulation. Also be sure to include any appropriate fabric pieces, such as one collar piece and a front flap piece.

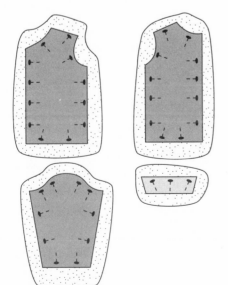

The coat pieces can be aligned in any direction because the grainline of the insulation is not important. Pin the pieces to the insulation. Cut quickly around each piece — you do not have to cut exactly along the fabric edges.

With a long stitch (7 to 8 stitches per inch), stitch around the edges of each coat piece, 1/8 in. from the seam line. (In other words, if the pattern has 5/8-in. seam allowances, stitch 1/2 in. from the fabric edge.) After stitching, carefully trim the excess insulation from the seam allowances.

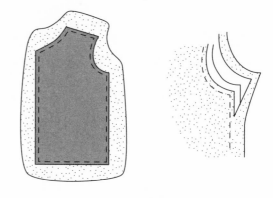

Next, quilt all the large pieces. With chalk or a marker, draw horizontal lines 12 in. apart, beginning at the middle of the piece. Stitch along each line, using a stitch length of 8 to 10 stitches per inch. Hold both the insulation and fabric taut as you stitch so that the layers do not shift between the quilting lines. (Some parts of the coat, such as the collar, usually have both sides cut from the coat fabric, and small or narrow pieces like these do not need to be quilted.)

Now assemble the coat or jacket according to the pattern directions.

OTHER DESIGN IDEAS

The basic duster-style coat can be modified in a multitude of ways. First decide what type of weather protection you want. For extreme conditions, make a waterproof or water-repellent insulated coat. For rain and wind protection, choose a lined or unlined coat made of waterproof or water-repellent fabric. This type of coat can also be worn over layers in colder weather. For wind and dust protection, use cotton fabrics, such as canvas. Make more fashionable coats out of denim, leather, or wool.

You might want to add fringe to a yoked duster. Or consider a denim duster with purchased fringe, or an all-leather duster.

You can add leather accents to a wool coat — collar, pocket flaps, elbow patches, or yoke trim.

Add a painted design to the back yoke of a duster with fabric paints, or sew on a decorative applique.

For trail riding, you can make a three-quarter-length rain slicker out of a lightweight waterproof fabric, such as coated nylon ripstop. Keep the coat as simple as possible to reduce weight and bulk, but keep the saddle gusset. The coat can be rolled up and fit into a small saddle bag.

CONVERTING A PATTERN INTO AN OUTBACK-STYLE COAT

You can easily adapt a simple raincoat pattern to make an outback-style coat. Choose a coat pattern with plain, straight lines. You'll add a rain cape, saddle gusset, elbow patches, leg straps, and handwarmer pockets (an extra piece with a side opening sewn on top of each pocket). These instructions assume that the coat is unlined.

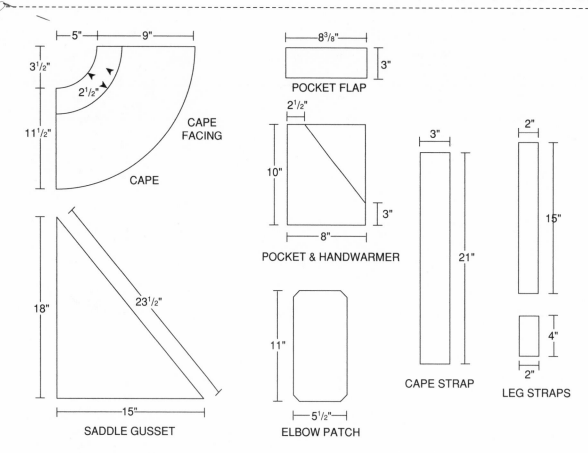

The dimensions for the pattern pieces are shown in the drawing. All seam allowances are $1/2$ in.

These pieces will fit most adult-size coats. For very large or very small coats, you might want to scale up or scale down the pockets and elbow patches. Pin these pieces to the coat pattern and hold them up to your body to decide how they look. The rain cape is another piece that might need adjustment. Match the shoulder seams of the coat front and back pieces. Match the center back of the rain-cape piece to the center back of the coat, remembering to allow for seam allowances. The center front of the rain cape should come to within roughly $2 1/2$ in. of the coat's center front. Also drape the rain cape over your shoulder to check the length. Some people like longer capes.

If you need to alter the rain cape, you can add width at center back, center front, and at the shoulder.

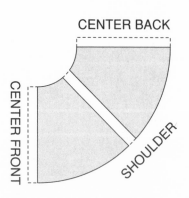

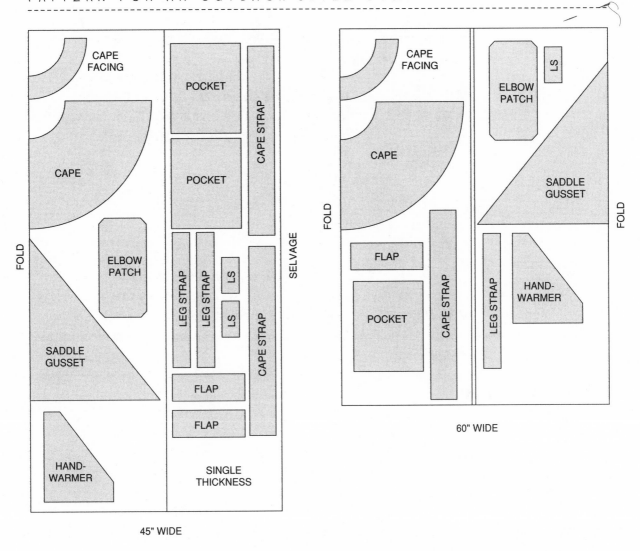

45" WIDE

60" WIDE

Yardage requirements could change if you alter any of the pieces.

Draw the pattern pieces on tissue or brown paper. If you can work on pattern paper with a 1-in. grid, drawing the pieces will be very easy. For the rain cape, draw the cape piece and then a separate facing piece for the cape. For the pocket, draw the pocket and than a separate handwarmer piece. For the elbow patch, draw the rectangle, mark 1 in. on either side of each corner, and then cut off the corners diagonally at the marks.

For 45-in.-wide fabric, you will need 1 1/4 yd. of extra fabric. For 60-in.-wide fabric, you will need 1 1/8 yd. of extra fabric. The layouts are shown in the drawing.

POCKET FLAP

Before doing anything else, make and sew on the pockets.

Pin the pocket flaps, with **right sides together**. Stitch around three of the sides, leaving a long side unstitched. Trim the seams, clip the corners, turn the pieces, and press. Topstitch.

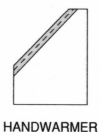

HANDWARMER

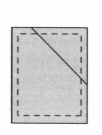

PLACE HANDWARMER ON POCKET

Finish the diagonal edges of the handwarmer. Pin the **wrong side** of the handwarmer to the **right side** of the pocket. Machine-baste 1/2 in. from all the pocket edges.

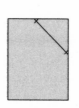

Fold the fabric under along the line of stitching and press. Bar-tack at the ends of the handwarmer opening.

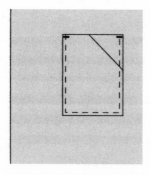

Pin the pockets to the front of the coat. They should be centered between the center front and side seams and below the waist. Hold up the front of the coat and check the position. Stitch around the bottom three edges of the pocket, and bar-tack at the ends of the stitching.

Pin the pocket flaps to the coat with the **right side** of the flap against coat and the raw edges of the flap aligned with the top edges of the pockets. Stitch. Trim the seams to a scant 1/4 in. and press the flaps over the pockets. Stitch 1/4 in. from first row of stitching, as shown in the drawing.

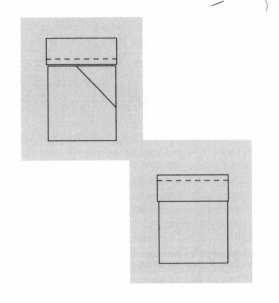

Continue with the construction of the coat until you're ready to sew the center back seam. (Don't make the sleeves — first you have to sew on the elbow patches, which will be the next step after this one.)

Sew the center back seam down to waist level.

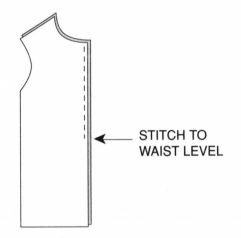

STITCH TO
WAIST LEVEL

Hem the long edge of the saddle gusset by turning it under 1/4 in., and then another 1/4 in., and stitching along the folded edge.

Mark a 1/2-in. seam line along the corners of the other two raw edges of the saddle gusset. Mark a dot at the intersection of the seam lines.

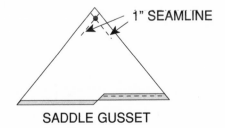

1" SEAMLINE

SADDLE GUSSET

With **right sides together**, pin one raw edge of the saddle gusset to one side of the center back below the seam. The dot on the gusset should be at the bottom of the center back seam. Stitch from the dot to the lower edge of gusset.

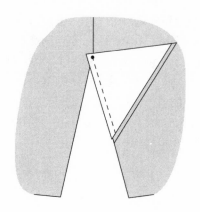

Pull the gusset around so that the remaining raw edge can be pinned to the remaining center back edge. Stitch from the dot to the lower edge of the gusset.

Clip the coat at the bottom of the saddle-gusset stitching. Finish the back-vent edges below the gusset by turning them under 1/4 in., and then another 1/4 in., and stitching along the folded edge.

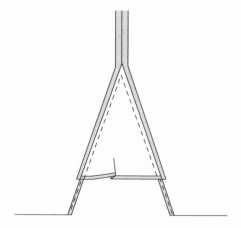

Stitch a rectangle at the top point of gusset. Install snap below gusset on the vent edges.

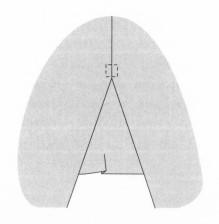

Turn under 1/2 in. of the edges of the elbow patches, and press. Pin the sleeve's underarm seam. Slip the sleeve onto your arm and determine the correct position of the elbow patch. Pin the elbow patch to the **right side** of the sleeve and try the sleeve on again.

ELBOW PATCH

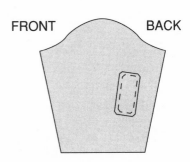

FRONT   BACK

When you're satisfied with the position of the elbow patch, unpin the underarm seam. Edgestitch the elbow patch to the sleeve. Repeat the process for the other sleeve. Finish constructing the coat

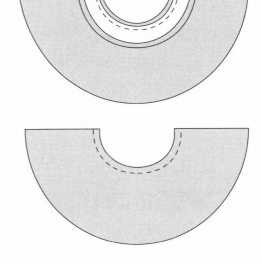

Finish the lower edge of the cape facing by turning it under 1/4 in., then another 1/4 in., and stitching along the folded edge. With **right sides together**, sew the cape facing to the neck edge of the cape. Clip the curves, turn the pieces, and press. Stitch 1/2 in. from the neck edge.

Finish the front edges and the hem of the cape by turning them under 1/4 in., then another 1/4 in., and stitching along the folded edges, as shown in the drawing. The front edges of the facing will be turned under with the front edge of the cape.

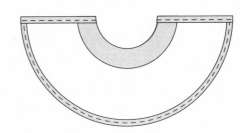

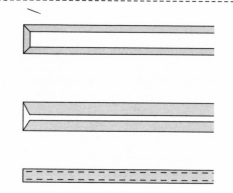

Turn all the edges of the cape straps under 1/4 in. and press. Fold the cape straps in half lengthwise, **wrong sides together**. Stitch around the edges.

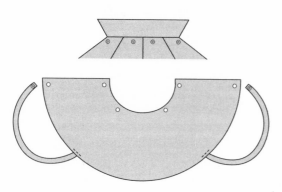

Now try on the coat and cape. Pin one end of each cape strap to the front corners of the cape. Loop the straps under your arms and pin them to the side backs of the cape. The loop of the straps should be slightly bigger than the coat armholes. Cut off any excess strap if necessary. Mark the strap positions on the back of the cape.

Sew one end of each strap to the wrong side of the cape at the marked positions. Install snaps to attach the front ends of the straps to the front corners of the cape. Install four snaps at the neck edge to attach the cape to the coat.

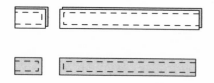

With **right sides together**, pin the front and back leg-strap pieces. Stitch three sides, as shown in the drawing. Trim the seams, clip the corners, turn the pieces, and press. Topstitch.

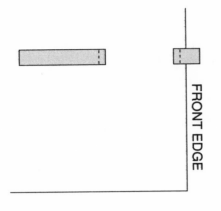

FRONT EDGE

Try on the coat again. Pin the leg straps on the inside of the coat slightly above knee level. The shorter strap goes to the front. Pin the straps together around your leg. There should be enough ease so that you can lift your leg to mount your horse. Mark the strap positions.

With the **right sides** of the straps against the **wrong side** of the coat, pin the straps as shown in the drawing. Stitch the raw edges of the straps to the coat.

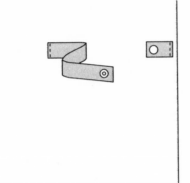

Trim the seam allowances and press the straps over the seams. Stitch 1/4 in. from the folded edges. Install the tops of the snaps on the ends of the front straps and the bottoms of the snaps on the ends of the back straps.

Install snaps in the coat front and the pocket flaps, at least 1/4 in. from the finished edges.

Appropriate Show Apparel

This appendix lists some basic guidelines for choosing proper show apparel, but the list is not all-inclusive. It's the competitor's responsibility to know what apparel is required by the rules and to know local fashions and conventions.

Hunter and Jumper Classes

The attire for hunter and jumper classes is quite traditional, and fashions do not change much from year to year. Color conventions for jackets and breeches can be slightly different for hunter-jumper shows than they are for breed shows.

1. A hunt coat with double-back vents in a solid dark color or with subtle pinstripes. The colors currently popular are navy blue, charcoal gray, dark hunter green, and black. Pinstripes should be no more than $1/16$ in. wide. For classes requiring formal hunt attire, women wear a dark-colored frock coat, shadbelly, or cutaway (a tailcoat whose front skirt curves back to the tails). Formal coats are usually worn with canary yellow vests; white or buff are less common.

2. A white or pastel shirt with a choker for women. A simple tie pin can be worn on the front of the choker.

For men, a white dress shirt is worn with a four-in-hand tie (a necktie tied with a slipknot), coordinated to match the color of the hunt coat.

3. Riding breeches with knee patches in light colors, such as light beige, buff, or pale gray. Competitors in some hunter classes, such as quarter horse classes, wear dark colors, such as rust and dark gray. White or pale-beige breeches are worn for Grand Prix jumper classes. Small children on ponies wear hunt jodhpurs in the same colors as breeches, with foot straps and leather garter straps.

4. Knee-high field or dress boots in black. Small children wear jodhpur boots with hunt jodhpurs. The jodhpur boots should be brown to match the garter straps.

5. Velvet-covered hunt cap, usually in black. Junior riders must wear protective headgear approved by the American Society for Testing Materials (ASTM) and secured with its attached harness. Women's hair should be neatly arranged, preferably pinned back or put up under the hat with a hairnet. Hats for formal hunt attire follow specific hunting traditions. Hunt caps are worn only by junior riders or the Master of the Hunt. Men and women wear hunting silk top hats. A bowler is worn with black coats. All hats worn with formal attire must have hat guards.

6. Dark gloves are recommended.

7. Spurs are optional.

8. Women should not wear jewelry of any kind. Even small stud earrings in pierced ears are considered unacceptable by some judges.

DRESSAGE CLASSES

Dressage attire is even more traditional than hunt attire. Basic hunt attire is perfectly acceptable up to Fourth Level, especially at schooling shows. At recognized shows, most competitors wear dressage coats and white or cream breeches.

1. In Training through Fourth Level classes: dark hunt coat or dressage coat. Above Fourth Level: dark shadbelly coat with hunt vest or attached vest points. Most coats worn for dressage are black, although for lower levels, any dark color is acceptable. Shadbellies are either black or midnight blue (very dark navy). Hunt vest or vest points worn with shadbellies are canary.

2. White shirt. Chokers are worn with hunt coats. With dressage coats and shadbellies, stock ties are worn. The stock tie should be attached with a simple gold tie pin.

3. Riding breeches in light colors. White is commonly worn with a black coat and cream with a midnight-blue coat. Light beige or light gray are also sometimes worn. Breeches with knee patches or full-seat inserts are both acceptable.

4. Knee-high dress boots in black.

5. Hunt cap with a hunt or dressage coat. Derby with dressage coat. Top hat with shadbelly. Women's derbies and top hats should be secured in place with bobby pins. Women's hair should be neatly arranged, preferably pinned back or put up under the hat with a hairnet.

6. Gloves are required. White are preferred, although black gloves are also acceptable at the lower levels.

7. Spurs are required above Fourth Level.

COMBINED TRAINING

Combined-training events require different attire for each phase — dressage, cross-country, and show jumping. At lower level competitions, the same attire can be worn for dressage and show jumping.

1. Attire for the dressage and show-jumping phases of a three-day event is the same as for dressage and jumper classes, respectively.

2. Breeches and tall boots worn with a polo shirt, turtle-neck, or pullover sweater for the cross-country phase. Back protector vests are recommended.

SADDLE-SEAT CLASSES

Saddle-seat attire is worn by riders of Saddlebreds, Tennessee Walkers, Morgans, Arabians, Racking Horses, and National Show Horses. Each organization has slightly different rules and conventions for different classes. General guidelines are:

1. Saddle suit or daycoat (women only) with jodhpurs. The saddle-suit coat has notched lapels and is worn with a matching vest and jodhpurs in conservative solid colors or subtle pinstripes. Earth tones and navy are good choices. The daycoat has a shawl collar and can be of a bright or light solid color. It is worn with dark pants. Sometimes a dark-colored or patterned vest is worn under the daycoat. After 6 P.M., a formal, tuxedo-style saddle-suit is sometimes worn. In addition, some saddle-seat classes (such as show hack) require shad-belly coats worn with breeches and tall boots.

2. A white or light shirt with a man's four-in-hand tie. A white shirt is always correct. Pastel shirts are also worn. The tie color should coordinate with the outfit or match the vest color. A tuxedo shirt and bow tie are worn with the formal suit.

3. Saddle-suit jodhpurs, also known as Kentucky jodh-purs, with knee reinforcements and boot straps. For informal and formal suits, the jodhpur color will match the coat. With daycoats, the jodhpurs will be a dark color that coordinates with the coat.

4. Jodhpur boots in black or brown to match the jodhpur color.

5. Women wear soft hats such as a derby, Homberg, or snap brim. Men wear Hombergs or snap brims.

Derbies worn with saddle suits match the color of the suit. Derbies worn with daycoats either match or contrast with the color of the coat. Hombergs and snap brims are usually black, dark brown, or dark blue. A grosgrain ribbon in the same color as the shirt can be wrapped around the hat band. Women's hats should be secured in place with bobby pins. Women's hair should be neatly arranged, preferably pinned back or put up under the hat with a hairnet. A bow can be worn on top of a bun to match the color of the horse's browband, cavesson, and girth.

6. Gloves are worn and should match the outfit.

7. A small boutonnière, matching the color of the horse's browband, can be worn on the lapel.

8. Subtle makeup is recommended for women. The lighting of indoor shows requires brighter makeup.

9. Equitation riders may not wear earrings, bracelets, or rings.

WESTERN SHOW CLASSES

Western show attire does not have as many hard-and-fast rules as the English disciplines. It is important to find out what is required and what is the current trend for your breed of horse and show class. Trends change quickly, so you need to stay informed so that you do not look dated. Basic guidelines are:

1. The American Horse Show Association (AHSA) specifies a long-sleeved shirt with buttons or snaps and collar. In addition, a necktie, kerchief, or bolo must be worn. The American Quarter Horse Association (AQHA) specifies a long-sleeved shirt with collar. Also worn by women competitors are shirts with vests, short jackets, and back-zippered blouses with stand-up collars. Male riders sometimes wear pullover sweaters. Because these options do not strictly follow the rules, it is up to the competitor to be aware of what is acceptable show attire.

2. Jeans, such as plain-style dark blue or black Wranglers, or black Western pants. In some classes, the pants match the color of the chaps. Belts are always worn, although not required. Match the belt color to the pants or chaps. Silver trophy buckles can be worn with the belt.

3. Chaps are required by the AHSA, although optional for AQHA classes. Most riders wear them. Only the shotgun style is worn. Most competitors wear fringed chaps, although in some cases scalloped chaps are appropriate.

4. Cowboy boots. The current style is the round-toed "roper" boots.

5. Western hat, usually of felt, though straw hats are sometimes worn by men in the summer. Styles of show hats are determined by the crease of the crown and the curve and the width of the brim. A currently popular style is a felt hat with a 4-in. brim, with little curve on the sides, and a wide, flat cattleman's crown. Felt hats are usually black or silverbelly, though they can also be colored to match the outfit. Women's hats should be secured in place with bobby pins. Women's hair should be neatly arranged, either pinned up under the hat or pulled back into a bun.

6. Gloves are optional, but should match the color of the shirt or jacket.

7. Women riders usually wear make-up.

8. Small earrings that do not dangle are acceptable. Earrings can match the color of the outfit or be gold or silver.

Sources of Supplies and Further Reading

Patterns

Fit For You
781 Golden Prados Drive
Diamond Bar, CA 91765
Tel: 909-861-5021

Send $1.00 for catalog.

Jean Hardy Pattern Co.
2151 La Cuesta Drive
Santa Ana, CA 92705
Tel: 714-544-1608

Send $1.00 for catalog.

Lola Gentry Originals
Box 5
Dell City, TX 79837

Send $3.00 for catalog.

SuitAbility
848 South Myrtle Avenue, Suite 5
Monrovia, CA 91016
Tel: 818-303-5730/ FAX: 818-303-1649

800
207-0256

Free catalog. Has over 50 patterns for riding apparel, including Western, saddle-seat, hunt-seat, dressage, and pleasure-riding attire. Also has patterns for horse clothing and equipment.

Sells several different types of stretch fabric for riding breeches and horse motif buttons.

OUTERWEAR FABRICS AND NOTIONS

(including gripper snaps and snap-setting tools)

Frostline Kits

2525 River Road
Grand Junction, CO 81505-2525
Tel: 800-548-7872

Send $2.00 for catalog.
Sells precut kits for down garments and other outerwear.
Some of their down coats can be used for riding. Also
sells fabrics, insulation, down, and notions.

The Green Pepper

3928 West 1st
Eugene, OR 97402
Tel: 503-345-6665

Send $2.00 for catalog.

Outdoor Wilderness Fabrics

16195 Latah
Nampa, ID 83651
Tel: 208-466-1602

Free price list.

The Rain Shed

707 NW 11th
Corvallis, OR 97330
Tel: 503-753-8900

Send $1.00 for catalog.

Other Fabrics and Notions

Allen Weaving Company

501 West Fayette Street
(Suite 222, Delavan Center)
Syracuse, NY 13204-2925
Tel/Fax: 315-475-4784

Sells oilcloth.

The Bee Lee Co.

P.O. Box 36108-S
Dallas, TX 75235-1108

Free catalog.

This company describes their products as "Sewing Supplies with a Western Accent." They sell many different kinds of snaps, including pearl snaps. Also a wide selection of notions and trims.

Designer Fabrics

2251 140th Avenue NE
Bellevue, WA 98005
Tel: 206-747-5200

Send $5.00 for wool-suiting swatches or $10.00 for silk-suiting swatches. Sells fabric for tailored riding coats.

Fashion Touches

P.O. Box 804
Bridgeport, CT 06604
Tel: 203-333-7738

Send $1.00 for order kit, redeemable with first order. Will custom-cover buttons with your fabric, suede, or leather.

Fields Fabrics

1695 44th Street SE
Grand Rapids, MI 49508
Tel: 800-67ULTRA or 616-455-4570

Send $10.00 (refundable with order) for 75 swatches of Ultrasuede and Ultraleather.
A good source of synthetic suedes and leather.

Jehlor Fantasy Fabrics

730 Andover Park West
Seattle, WA 98188
Tel: 206-575-8250

Send $3.50 for catalog ($2.50 refundable on first order). Send SASE for information on swatching service. Sells specialty fabrics, such as sequinned fabrics, brocades, lames, satins, and metallics.

LEATHER AND LEATHERWORKING SUPPLIES

Berman Leathercraft, Inc.
25 Melchor Street
Boston, MA 02210
Tel: 617-426-0870

D'Anton
3079 NE Oasis Road
West Branch, IA 52358
Tel: 319-643-2568

The Leather Factory
P.O. Box 50429
3847 E. Loop 820 South
Ft. Worth, TX
Tel: 800-433-3201 or 817-496-4874
(Or check phone book for local store.)

Tandy Leather Company
P.O. Box 2934
Fort Worth, TX 76113
(Or check phone book for local store)

Weaver Leather
P.O. Box 68
Mt. Hope, OH 44660
Tel: 800-932-8371

BOOKS AND MAGAZINES

The Busy Woman's Sewing Book and *Ten, Twenty, Thirty Minutes to Sew* by Nancy Ziemen.

Nancy's Notions
P.O. Box 683
Beaver Dam, WI 53916-0683
Tel: 800-833-0690

These books contain many useful sewing tips that will improve and speed up your sewing of riding clothes.

Also watch Nancy Ziemen's PBS television show, "Sewing With Nancy." Videos of her show are available in libraries. She also sells a wide selections of notions. Free catalog.

Easy, Easier, Easiest Tailoring by Pati Palmer and Susan Pletsch.

Palmer/Pletsch Associates
P.O. Box 8422
Portland, OR 97207

This book is my "bible" for making tailored coats. I still refer to it whenever I make one.

How to Sew Leather, Suede, Fur by Phyllis W. Schwebke and Margaret B. Krohn.

Macmillan Publishing Company
866 Third Avenue
New York, NY 10022

Although this book is primarily about sewing all-leather garments, it thoroughly covers all aspects of sewing with leather.

Sewing Activewear and *Tailoring* by the Singer Sewing Reference Library.

Cy DeCosse Incorporated
5900 Green Oak Drive
Minnetonka, MN 55343
Tel: 800-328-3895

Also available in many fabric stores. These books contain beautiful photographs and lots of useful advice. *Sewing Activewear* is useful if you're making riding tights, riding sweatpants, or riding outerwear.

Shirtmaking by David Coffin.

Taunton Press
63 South Main Street
Newtown, CT 06470

Everything you need to know to fit and assemble a professionally finished custom-made shirt. Lots of detailed information on constructing collars and cuffs. Accompanying videotape also available.

Show Grooming: The Look of a Winner by Charlene Strickland, 2nd Edition.

Breakthrough Publications, Inc.
310 North Highland Ave.
Ossining, NY 10562

In addition to extensive information on grooming and turnout, this book has an excellent chapter on show apparel for all major breeds and disciplines. It gives detailed information on all aspects of show attire.

Horse and Rider Magazine
Practical Horseman Magazine

Cowles Magazines, Inc.
Tel: 800-435-9610

Horse and Rider periodically has articles about show apparel for Western classes. *Practical Horseman* runs articles about correct apparel for hunters, jumpers, dressage, and eventing.

Sew News

PJS Publications, Inc.
Box 3134
Harlan, IA 51537-3134

Although this magazine has many useful articles about sewing, it is also an excellent reference for mail-order sources of fabrics and notions. Just about every sewing-related company advertises in this magazine. It is available in most fabric stores.

PATTERN PIECES

ZIPPER POCKET

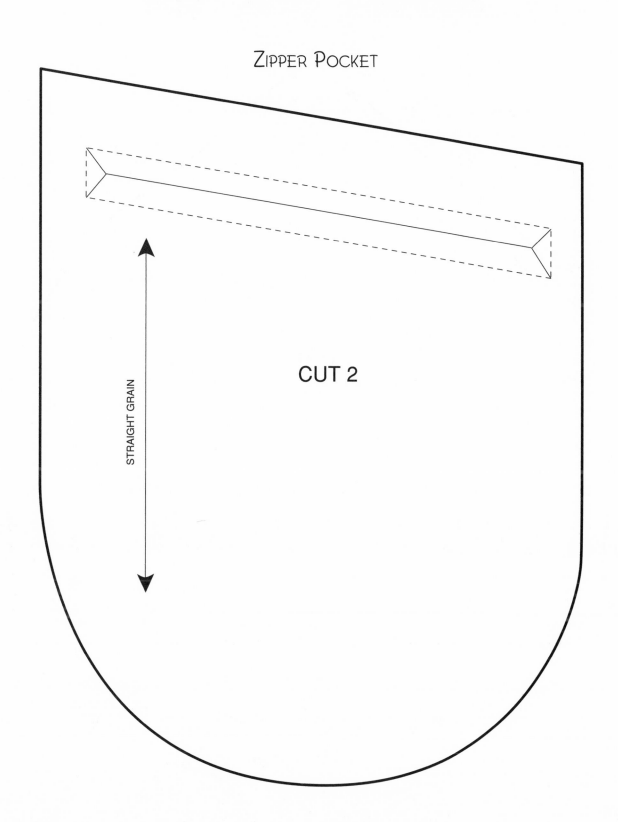

CUT 2

STRAIGHT GRAIN

KNEE PATCH (UPPER)

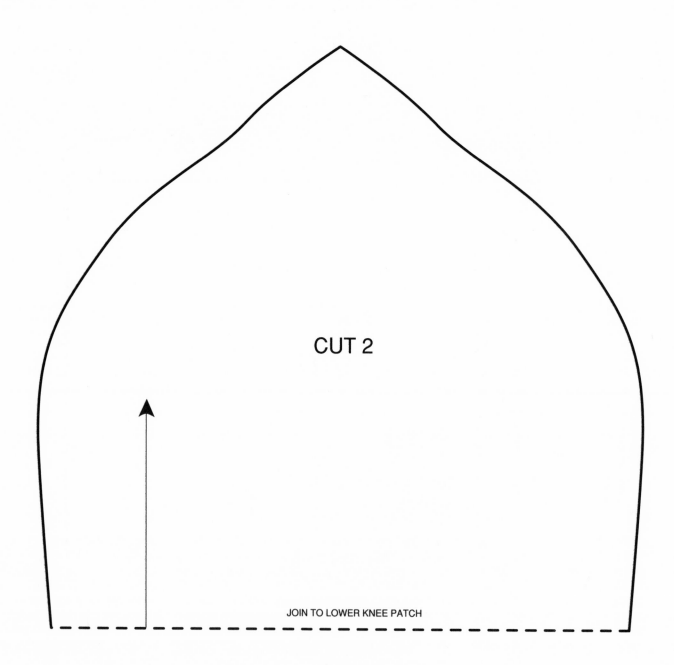

CUT 2

JOIN TO LOWER KNEE PATCH

KNEE PATCH (LOWER)

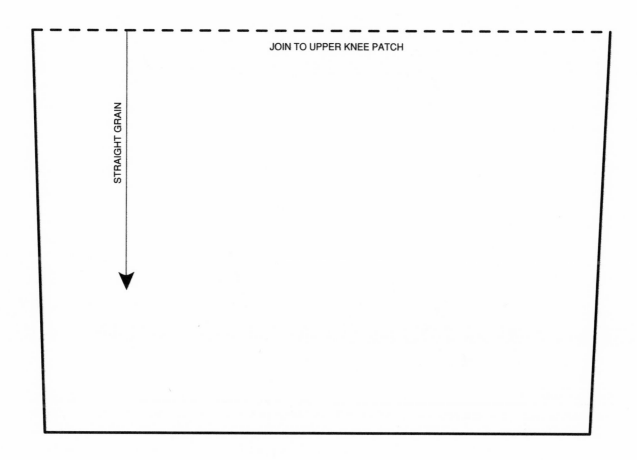

JOIN TO UPPER KNEE PATCH

STRAIGHT GRAIN

CHOKER

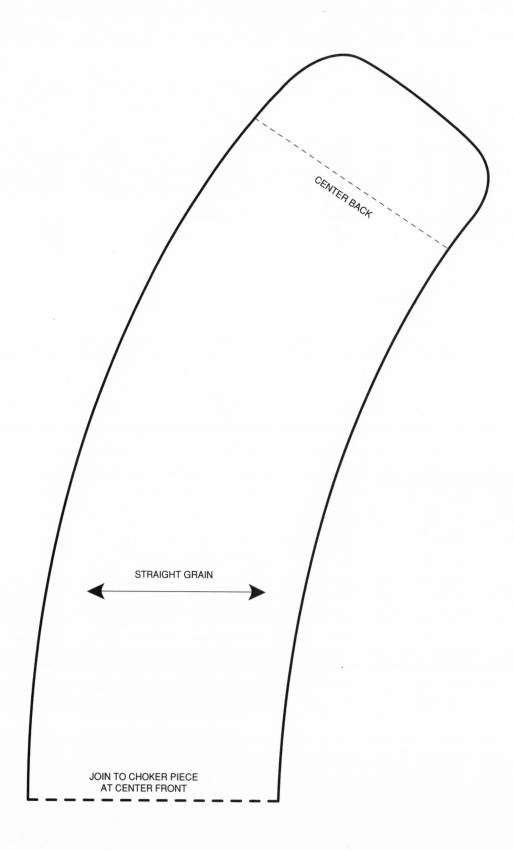

CENTER BACK

STRAIGHT GRAIN

JOIN TO CHOKER PIECE
AT CENTER FRONT

CENTER FRONT

CHOKER
SIZE 15 NECK

CUT 2 FABRIC
CUT 1 INTERFACING

CENTER BACK

INDEX